Seeds of Devotion

Weekly Contemplations On Faith

ROGER BUTTS

An Imprint for GracePoint Publishing
(www.GracePointPublishing.com)

GracePoint Matrix, LLC
322 N Tejon St. #207
Colorado Springs CO 80903
www.GracePointMatrix.com
Email: Admin@GracePointMatrix.com
SAN # 991-6032

Library of Congress Control Number: 2021900957
ISBN-13: (Paperback)# 978-1-951694-36-4
eISBN: (eBook)# 978-1-951694-35-7

Artwork used by permission and courtesy of Norah Fioriti Butts

Books may be purchased for educational, business, or sales promotional use.
For bulk order requests and price schedule contact:
Orders@GracePointPublishing.com

Table of Contents

Endorsements

In *Seeds of Devotion*, Roger Butts masterfully weaves together dramatic stories and prayers born out of a career as a front-line hospital chaplain, pastor and community organizer. The stories are poignant, insightful and down-right inspiring. But he also combines them with the timeless wisdom of both the Hebrew and New Testament texts, and guidance from the Buddha, Rumi, Thomas Merton, Henri Nouwen and many others. Seeds is written in language that is casual yet personal enough to feel you are hearing the advice of a friend. The prayers that help frame each chapter are both original and worthy of reflection. The prayers themselves are a treasure.

And the questions posed after each chapter left me haunted. When I felt exiled, what brought me back to center? How have I accompanied the frail and the weak? What is my relationship to silence? How have I been put through fire? How do I see myself as a healing presence?

Seeds of Devotion is written to guide each of us to face these challenging times by holding fast to the goodness already present within each of us. That is exactly what Roger reveals for so many people day after day.

- Martin Doblmeier -
Emmy Award winning documentary filmmaker
(*The Power of Forgiveness, Bonhoeffer,*
and *Chaplains* among others)

Roger Butts's new book, Seeds of Devotion, is an invitation to begin or deepen a meditative, mindful stance in the reader's daily life. Consisting of 52 meditations which conclude with a prayer and reflective questions, it provides an encounter of the Spirit with the spirit of Jesus, Muhammad, the Buddha, as well as the spirit of wisdom figures such as Thomas Merton and Dorothy Day. Writing in evocative prose that borders on the poetic, Roger Butts unites ancient wisdom with contemporary insights, encouraging a devotion that is profoundly inclusive of many cultures and ages in time. His book is rich for the spirit in all of us that waits to be awakened.

- Ed Sellner
is professor emeritus of theology and spirituality at St. Catherine University in St. Paul, Minnesota where he taught for 35 years, and is a spiritual writer and guide. Author of numerous books, his most recent are *Celtic Saints and Animal Stories: A Spiritual Kinship* and *Pilgrimage: Exploring a Great Spiritual Practice.*

In this book, readers will find a wise companion for the journey of life. Drawing on stories of courageous faith, scripture, and his own life as a pastor and chaplain, Roger Butts shares and invites deep reflection on life's primary questions and hopes.

- Jake Morrill,
Executive Director,
Unitarian Universalist Christian Fellowship

Roger Butts has an incredible capacity for weaving goodness and beauty together against the cold, hard reality of human suffering. He brings ancient truth to life in a tapestry that rides on the cutting edge of tomorrow, taking us from where we've been to right where we need to be. He is an impeccable guide pointing the way to life in all its messiness and wonder. Relax. You're in good hands now.

- Kim Holman,
Founder, Contemplative Light

In these pages you will find the beautiful wisdom of an open-heart. Honest and vulnerable, Roger Butts puts words to the life of prayer and helps us see the divine in the changes and chances of life.

**- The Rev. Jeremiah Williamson - Rector,
Grace and St. Stephen's Episcopal Church,
Colorado Springs**

A few years ago, Rev. Roger Butts gifted me with a devotional he created, much like this one. By reading the reflections, immersing myself in the poems, and praying the prayers, I was able to open and heal my exhausted heart. I am so excited that he has created this devotional for the world to share. Roger has a unique perspective on life that allows him to both gather and bring forth profound wisdom and make it accessible. In order to compile such a collection of thoughts, invocations and adorations as you will find in this book, a person must first successfully traverse many of life's most challenging circumstances. Roger has walked the path of love, courage and forgiveness. The value of what he learned along the way blesses every page. This is a book to be loved, treasured and revisited for many years to come. I am so pleased to recommend it!

**- Rev. Dr. Ahriana Platten,
Unity Spiritual Center**

A beautifully powerful book of stories and journeys, personal and universal and timeless, punctuated with generous offerings of prayers and reflections, providing encouragement and enrichment for all who journey. Roger has a true gift for speaking from the heart—vulnerable, raw and real—and in doing so, you find he's right by your side, meeting you where you are, speaking directly into your heart, as a genuine friend and spiritual companion.

**- Andrew Palmer,
Sensei - teacher in The Open Source Zen tradition**

Preface

Your life is dripping with the divine presence. The world is dripping with the divine presence. No matter how dire the situation or joyous the occasion, we are invited into the awareness of that beloved presence.

There are different things needed to get there: humility and self-awareness (St Teresa of Avila), walking the dog for an hour and a half (my wife), yoga, centering prayer. Silence is crucial. Naming your experience. A prayerful orientation. And asking the right questions to alight your imagination and compassion.

This book is an attempt to help us get there. I, for one, like the idea of having a lot of different voices from a lot of different times and circumstances to help guide us. Some voices you'll know. Some you won't, like the old dying woman on the fourth floor whose last words to me were, "Thank you God for everything."

All the stories are an attempt to enflame your heart: to quiet your mind and help you to enter into the great mystery.

This book invites you to ask big questions of your own life, so that the text of your life becomes a gospel, a sharing of the good news that is the wisdom that lives in your heart and soul and mind and body. We get to that good news—born of struggle, triumph, loneliness, fear, grief, and above all, love—only in the silence. "The silence is all there is," Annie Dillard reminds us. This book is an attempt to help you see the wisdom of your life, in all of its components and busyness, by showing you stories that help guide the way to a life of the spirit.

Here you will find little snippets, little snapshots of life, the life that is here and now, followed by a prayer. And closing out with journal questions and conversation starters. The reflections are short. They are designed to read in a short amount of time. To paint a picture, to cast a vision, to suggest a little something. The prayers are designed to soothe your soul, to provide comfort and peace, and occasionally challenge. The questions are designed to linger with you throughout the week. When you are driving or stuck in traffic or embracing a moment of quiet in your home or on a walk, you can ask yourself: What is my image of the divine? Where did I find grace this week?

In my work as a hospital chaplain, I sit and let the space open up in the room so that the patient or the family member or the caregiver can speak from the deepest part of themselves. Often tears come. Often, very often, laughter comes. Of course, stories. So many stories. When I left parish ministry to become a chaplain, a parishioner gave me a poster: *The World is Made of Stories*. I believe it.

Sometimes, a patient will look at me and say, "I have no one who listens to me. Thank you for listening."

These reflections. These questions. These prayers. They are all designed to help *you* listen. To the deep wisdom at the very heart of your heart. And to connect. With your true authentic self, warts and all. To your beloved ones. And to the holy, whose love is never far from you.

Enjoy. Listen to your good news. Listen to your pain. Listen to your lonely spots. Explore. Pray. Talk. Let the silence keep you and speak out of that place.

Take these slow. Even though they are short little pieces, the idea is to let them sit with you throughout the week. There are about 52 reflections (story, prayer, journal questions). Sit with them. Let them sink in.

Throughout the book, there are little interruptions that I've called Deep Dives. In fact, the very first story is a deep dive. And those are little stories that do not have a prayer or a journal question. They are just stand-alone reflections. Take time with those too.

One more invitation. Recently, with the COVID-19 pandemic, we have experienced an odd, disturbing kind of social dislocation. Restaurants and coffee shops are take-out only. Faith communities, often gather via Zoom instead of in person. Hugging is a bit of a no-no. So take these journal questions and think of them also as conversation starters. Get to know the folks you are closest to in new ways, with new questions and new avenues of connection. Take curiosity and courage with you into these questions, into these stories, and on the other side you'll find compassion. For yourself and others.

This book is dedicated to ones who listen to me with loving hearts: My wife Marta. Our kids Norah, Nick and Nina.

Special thanks to Contemplative Light who published a number of these prayers and reflections at contemplativelight.org. Special thanks to the Unitarian Universalist Christian Fellowship. I am a member of a tiny caucus within a tiny denomination. But they are mine and I love them. Thanks to Skinner House Books, who published a few of these essays and prayers. Thanks to the good folks at GracePoint Publishing: Michelle Vandepas, who believed in me way before this book came out; my coach, Karen Parker; and my editor, Laurie Knight, who made this readable and who could have written this book a thousand times better.

And all the ones, of so many different denominations, who sat in church classes and said: I'm here to deepen. I am here because I feel disconnected. I am here to explore and question in a place of non-anxious loving presence. Without their wisdom and courage, I wouldn't have collected these stories.

Roger Butts
2nd week of Advent, 2020
In the deep pines of the Black Forest,
Colorado

Dedication

With every breath I plant the seeds of devotion
I am a farmer of the heart.
–Rumi

For Marta, Norah, Nicholas, and Nina
With gratitude to Carl Sandburg, who gave me a song
and Thomas Merton, who gave me a map

Foreword

Chaplains have one of the most challenging roles in the world of ministry. I myself have never served as a chaplain, but I have been ministered to by several chaplains over the years and I have been privileged to call a few chaplains friends. What I always see when I meet a chaplain is a person who is available to encounter life at the frontier of mystery, the place where we encounter death, or suffering, or trauma. And unlike a minister or rabbi or priest who has their own flock to care for, chaplains face a unique challenge in that their "congregation" is the ever-shifting population of people in hospitals, emergency rooms, hospice care, or other challenging circumstances. This means the chaplain is often meeting, listening to, and caring for people they have literally just met—and immediately brought into the depth of that person's (or their family's) grief, loss, or fear.

I don't care what religious label you might wear or what spiritual path (if any) that you follow: as human beings we have some qualities in common that cannot be divided by our culture or creed. We will all age, unless death meets us early in life. We all suffer, sooner or later. We all experience loss in some form or fashion. And as Jim Morrison of The Doors reminds us in a very blunt way, "No one here gets out alive"—we will most assuredly die, and most of us will leave behind grieving loved ones when we do.

This may not be a pleasant topic to contemplate, but it is the honest-to-heaven truth, and so it is something we all must reckon with. Indeed, for centuries monks in the Christian tradition have had a little motto that some people might think morbid, but to the monks themselves it is an invitation to freedom: *memento mori*, remember that one day you, too, must die.

So how do we find meaning and purpose in the awe-inspiring mysteries of life? How do we make sense of suffering, navigate grief, and make peace with the fact that death is a part of life? And, since it is not my purpose here just to wallow in the shadow side of life, how do we also make room for the great joys that life can bring us, from love to pleasure to meaning to the urge to create?

These are questions that have inspired philosophers, poets, shamans, wisdom-keepers, saints, and mystics down the centuries. And these questions echo in this rich and eclectic collection of meditations from chaplain Roger Butts. Roger first embraced the good work of chaplaincy as a relatively young person, working part time in a hospital to put himself through divinity school. Although he has logged in time as the minister of a couple of Unitarian-Universalist communities, eventually he was called back in to chaplaincy work, where he continues to serve.

Like many chaplains, Roger is a natural storyteller, and he is able — while protecting the confidentiality and anonymity of the people he serves — to invite us in to the liminal space of the chaplain, where he encounters people of many different faiths and many different temperaments. He has been a front-line witness to miracles and to tragedies, and he has stories to tell that will fill you with hope, inspire you, startle you, and even break your heart.

But he is not *just* a storyteller, even though he has quite a gift there. Roger is a myth-maker, a weaver of meaning and understanding, someone who knows how to extract a sense of connection between the events he might encounter in this life, and the collective wisdom of the world. He draws on sources as diverse as Rumi, Thomas Merton, the Buddha, the Desert Fathers, the Qu'ran, and the American Civil Rights Movement. Although his center of gravity is the Christian tradition, his Christianity is open, inclusive, welcoming, and passionately committed to justice.

What I love about this book is that it's really three books in one. Paired with each of Roger's insightful meditations is a prayer, often in poetic form, and a series of reflection questions. It's all structured in a format similar to the ancient monastic practice of *lectio divina* or sacred reading. We are invited to read and reflect on the meditation itself, to respond prayerfully through Roger's prayer, and then to ponder on the questions that invite us to make the heart of the meditation our own.

Roger understands that the best spirituality is always incarnational: it's not a flight from the body into some abstract headspace, but the Spirit (whose name means "Breath") always invites us back into our bodies, back into the stuff and matter of our lives. We encounter God right here, right now, in our bodies, in our breath, in whatever is happening in our lives: pain or pleasure, joy or suffering, loss or opportunity. By weaving together prayer, meditation, and thought-provoking questions, this book invites us not only into the wisdom of Roger's world, but even more importantly, it calls us back to encounter the wisdom of our own.

- Carl McColman
- Author of *The Big Book of Christian Mysticism,*
Encountering Silence and *Unteachable Lessons*

Lord of the Dance

Seek refuge in thy soul; have there thy heaven! Bhagavad-Gita

I want you to imagine walking into a palatial stone cathedral. As you enter the foyer, your eyes take in all the beauty, the majesty. And you look up.

Above you, in this circular foyer, is a frieze cut into the stone. And you see that there are figures, and not just figures, but figures dancing, laughing, and enjoying one another's company.

Oh, you look more closely. The old timey figure is labeled *Saint Paul* and the one holding a big staff is labeled *Moses* and there is *John the Baptist.* You think *Okay, pretty typical church stuff here.* But then you see Martin Luther King and dancing next to him, Malcolm X. Across the way is Harriet Tubman, her face wrinkled with work and wisdom. Is that kid Ryan White? Yes. And is that Harvey Milk? *It is.* And there is Saint Francis and his sister Saint Clare and a bunch of birds. You are intrigued.

There's the Buddha and there's Muhammad and you see at the center of it all, a laughing, dancing Jesus. Lord of the dance.

What beauty, what inspiration! And you see that there are empty spaces up there, waiting for the next figure to be chiseled upon the frieze.

It's Tuesday afternoon. You light a candle and you go in to pray.

O God, what part of me belongs on that frieze? O God, who would I place on that frieze? Thank you for the peacemakers, thank you for the visionaries. Thank you for the part of me that longs to be like those folks. Convert me, O God. Make me a new creation.

And you sit in silence. And maybe you hear or feel a response.

The voice of the Spirit. The voice of Lady Wisdom whispering in your ear: *You are precious in my sight. You are not famous and you won't make this particular frieze, but you'll make someone's. You are a peacemaker. You are a visionary. You are a good gift. You are my beloved. And I will use you just as I used those folks, to make the world a better place.*

You, too, are a good gift. No doubt. And let's ask the question directly: *Which part of you belongs on that frieze?*

Take my friend, Annie. She has decided to adopt a child with Oppositional Defiant Disorder, a child who lashes out all the time, because she has lived with trauma—deep trauma—all her nine years. Annie adopted her and is just patiently raising her. She has selflessly given up her easy living and is now parenting a child who may or may not grow beyond the trauma. Maybe Annie should be on the wall.

Or my friend Robert, who supported a student going through a very difficult choice: After having been rejected by her top school, choosing between Wichita and Dallas were almost paralyzing following her grave disappointment. She felt as though she were a failure, and that she hadn't other options, but he was there for her. He had no obligation to her. Robert listened, holding space for her to vent. Let's put him on the frieze. He always seems to do this for people.

What about you? Look at your qualities that other people see in you. In what ways are you like the Buddha or Jesus? Let's celebrate those. Let's feed those qualities, water them, and nurture them. Make them stronger.

And those empty spaces or incomplete faces upon the frieze? Who would you put up there? Who is worthy to dance with those we hold in the highest?

New Name

*You'll get a brand-new name straight from the mouth of God.
You'll no more be called Forsaken, but you will be called, My delight
is in her. God delights in you. Adapted from Isaiah 62:4-5*

After the long exile in Babylon, the people returned home. And Isaiah proclaimed the good news: *You've got a new name.* Consider the exile. The exhaustion of it. The pure grief. The disorientation. Imagine how that must have been. After not being able to sing their holy songs for so long, finally, finally, some hope. Finally, the arrival of a new thing. In this remarkable passage, the people of Israel have a new name: *My Delight is In Her.* Previously, their name was desolate, forsaken, ones who were in exile, but now they are *The Ones I Delight In.* *See the entire story of the exile in Babylon in Jeremiah 39-43. To see an emotional response to the exile, read Psalm 137 or the Book of Lamentations.

Think of the moment your child first called you *Mom* or *Dad*, or your niece called you *Uncle* or *Aunt*. When you're beloved called you *beloved.* When your bestie for life called you *friend.* In those moments, you realized something fundamentally new about yourself. You saw yourself with new eyes. How much must those Israelites have learned about themselves when going from the name *forsaken, lost, exiled,* to *The Ones In Whom I Delight.* Imagine the relief! Hold in your heart what that must have felt like!

Consider the exile. The people were forcibly removed from their land and taken to Babylon, where they were unable to freely engage in the rituals that give their people meaning. Ripped from the place they called home. Unable to worship their God. They were captives, crying out, "How can we sing our songs in this foreign land?" But the exile ended, they returned and they made their way back, and God said, *I haven't forgotten you. You were in a bad place, your name was Desolate, but now you are home, and your name will be You Are My Great Delight.* And they remembered the covenant that they had with God. They committed themselves to welcoming the stranger, taking care of the orphans and the widows, making sure the poor among them have enough food, and restoring the temple. They had new life, a new name, and they thrived.

This is a profound passage of new birth, new beginnings. It is about transformation. As they were marching into exile, the rabbis said, "God was marching with them. Crying out with them. *My shoulders are heavy. My back stings. My knees buckle.*"

God was hurting *with* God's people. But once the exile was over, Delight, and Love, and Transformation permeated the air. And a new name was upon them. A new name comes with new life! Who among us hasn't had to start over again, who among us hasn't felt the sting of exile? Maybe some of us are in the throes of exile, even now. Isaiah reminds us that this sense of exile is not the end of the story. God's got a new name for each one of us, waiting for us to claim it. *Beloved Child, You Are My Delight*, is a new name—maybe even yours.

Did you ever hear that old spiritual, "I've Got a New Name Over in Zion?" Zion starts here. It begins here. Your new name awaits you, in the kingdom of God, on earth as it is in heaven, the beloved community. Your name might be *Grace*. You might *be the one who is full of joy. The one whose heart is generous. The one who will not give up. The one who clings to hope. The one who helps. The one who radiates Light.* You might be any number of new names representing your heart of hearts.

Whoever you are, you are also the one in whom God delights, beloved child of love, beloved child of God. Find your name and live into it. Breathe life into your new name!

Prayer

Fellow Sojourner, Spirit of Life,
Light in the darkness, One beyond all names,

Walk with us. Walk beside us.
Give strength to our legs,
courage to our hearts,
vision to our eyes.

When we are all alone, or feel so,
When we don't know what the next day will bring,
When we can't quite sing our holy songs,
remind us, O God, that you have a special name,
a new name just for each one of us.

A name we can claim as our own,
Love Incarnate,
Builder of Dreams,
Hope in All Things,
whatever our names,
give us occasion,
again, and again,
to claim that name
and to live into it.

Amen.

Reflection Questions

What name will you take on for yourself in this period of time? For example, a friend of mine retired from the military after 24 years of service. He was no longer a soldier. He struggled to know who he was, since it was clear who he wasn't. Still in service, but no longer a warrior, he held onto the name *servant*. He was still devoted and loyal, he just needed a new place to fit in. He had the servant's heart, and he sought guidance into where he might be of future service. He held on to the word *servant* to guide him through his transition out of the military. What name would you like to breathe life into at this time? What name represents the Divine's intention for you?

In the Beloved Community, what is the name that the holy one has for you?

What name do you wish to claim?

Consider the word *exile*. It's the state of being barred from a group/community/nation where you belong. We belong in joy, for example. We are meant to live in joy. Consider a time when you may have been kept from joy. Was it the loss of a loved one? Was it a depression that robbed you of the ability to find joy in those dark days? When have you experienced a form of exile? When you have been in exile, what has brought you back to your center, your land, your heart? What was that like and how did that happen?

Thank you, God, for Everything

Give us this day our daily bread.
Jesus. The Gospel of Matthew 6:11

It was a Friday night, just after dinner. I was at the hospital. My work was slowing down; most people don't need to see a hospital chaplain after 7 p.m. unless there is a really powerful reason.

Then my pager went off. A nurse on the fourth floor said to me, "Roger, there is a patient up here, an older woman. She is going to hospice on Saturday, but tonight she is terribly confused and I think she could use a visit."

"Of course. I'll be right there."

I looked at my phone to check the time: *in two hours I'd be off.* Truth be told, I was ready for the weekend.

As I was about to enter the room, the nurse told me, "She's been saying the Lord's Prayer, over and over."

I gathered myself outside the room and said a silent little prayer to center myself. I walked in.

She was definitely an old woman, frail and weak, ready to give in to that great mystery. As a hospital chaplain I've walked into rooms like this many times. The feeling is palpable, a deep, abiding quiet. Often there is a profound peace, in this case made even greater because the patient was entirely alone, a rarity in such cases. Often, I enter a room full of family and friends, buzzing around, trying to fill the last few moments with memories turned to chatter. This was different.

As I approached, I noticed that the nurse was right. The woman was saying the Lord's Prayer. I held her hand. Eventually I joined her in reciting it. Her voice was weak so I whispered alongside her. *Give us this day our daily bread. And forgive us our trespasses.*

As we approached the end of the Lord's Prayer, she noticed my presence. She looked at me through cloudy, peace-filled eyes and smiled gently. "I can't seem to remember the ending," she said. "But, oh well. Thank you, God, for everything."

And with that, she entered a gentle sleep. After a while of holding her hand I simply walked out of the room with a new ending for a prayer that I love.

 Prayer

First, walk gently.

You're entering into the great mystery.

Sorrow, regret, anger, grief, relief.
You never know what you'll find.

You may as well walk gently into that room,
which will likely be dark and quiet.

Second, talk gently.
The dead dream.
And the survivors do too.

They are in a fog,
or out to sea,
or in the deep woods.
Pick your image.

But talk gently, that mystery
will one day be you and yours.

Third, act gently.
Your gentleness
will invite whatever needs to happen
to happen.
If at all possible,
make it so the wife/husband/
mother/child
Hardly knows you are there.

Listen gently.
Listen with your eyes
and your ears
and mostly your heart.
The stories will come.
Be there to hear them.
Stories remind the wife
that she still is alive
And is alone and is not alone
all at once.

Be the Spirit
or Jesus
or Muhammad
or the Buddha

Pick your guide and be that person.

Mary. Dorothy Day.
Thomas Merton.
It matters not.

Of course, *you* are the best option.
So be you, in all of your quirky,
unexpected, beautiful, flawed,
perfect essence.

Amen.

How have you accompanied the frail, the weak, the very vulnerable? What did you do? What part of you emerged that was a surprise?

How has another accompanied you in a difficult time? What do you remember and what seemed to help?

Who are your guides and what do they teach you?

Carl Scovel Saved My Life

*O sing unto the LORD a new song; Sing unto
the LORD, all the earth. Psalm 96*

arl Scovel saved my life. Well, more accurately, a single paragraph referred to as The Great Surmise of forty-five words
written by Carl Scovel in a four-hundred-page book, *A
Unitarian Universalist Christian Reader* (1996-97, Vol. 51, 52), saved
my life.

I'll explain.

In 2002, I was called to be the minister at the Unitarian Church,
in Davenport, Iowa. There, my wife and I had three children, good
friends, an amazing community. I knew successes. Among other
things, we started a community organizing group called Progressive
Action for the Common Good where we brought together local
interfaith clergy groups on many issues, local and national. Within
this group, we grew from simple support for the LGBTQIA+ community to performing legally binding same-sex weddings. It was certainly progressive, but it didn't come without challenge.

While in Davenport, I also experienced difficulties around the art
and science of being a senior minister. I was scattered and unable to
focus. I engaged in struggles with people I imagined weren't on board.
I was sensitive to criticism. I grew depressed. I did not know how to
re-birth my ministry in Davenport. I felt like a change of scenery
might do me good.

I took a call at a church in Colorado Springs. The baggage I brought with me there grew heavier. Things only got tougher and more complicated by 2012 at my second church in Colorado Springs. My shortcomings collided with a congregation that was not a good fit for me, as I was not for them.

After eleven years, my time as a senior minister was over. Who was I if not a senior minister?

After leaving parish ministry, I entered into dark, difficult times. The "dark night of the soul" is nothing new, but when it is yours, it sure feels exhausting, enduring, excruciating. I wavered between cynicism and despair, wondering how much I could take. And all those books about learning to walk in the dark are right: You learn things in the dark that you'd never discover otherwise.

My wife, my friends, and fellow clergy (UU and otherwise) were helpful. One thing that enabled me to move forward was my faith: my strange, hybrid, Unitarian Universalist Christianity. My faith faltered occasionally. It took some hits. It bent in strong winds. It roared. It whispered. It disappeared occasionally. It adjusted, adapted, found new avenues, made new inroads. That whole post-resignation time period was one big heartache, and it required all the resilience I could muster.

In such times, you learn about what abides. The thing I returned to over and over was a single paragraph I had preached on many times over the years. I discovered this single paragraph from Carl Scovel in the mid to late 90s in a huge volume put out by the Unitarian Universalist Christian Fellowship. That essay was one of more than three dozen in the book. This particular paragraph was like a needle in a haystack, but I swear it was as if it were written to me in neon and flashing off the pages, *just to me.*

That paragraph saved me in that time. I found it comforting. I found it challenging. I found it life-affirming. And it was the constant in the storm. It was lighthouse and life jacket. It showed me the path home. This paragraph:

The Great Surmise says simply this: At the heart of all creation lies a good intent, a purposeful goodness, from which we come, by which we live our fullest, to which we shall at last return. And this is the supreme reality of our lives.

If it was true of all creation that there was "a good intent, a purposeful goodness, through which we could live our fullest," most authentic lives. It was true of me too. I was part of the goodness. I was part of that supreme reality, even if my identity as a senior minister of a tradition I loved was no longer true. Something else was true, even so, I could *be* that goodness. I could live out of that goodness. And I could reimagine my life, with that image seared into my soul.

Sometime in the 1990s, somewhere in Washington, D.C., when I was alternating between All Souls Church and Universalist National Memorial Church, I discovered this essay ("Beyond Spirituality") along with the UU Christian Fellowship. Coincidentally, I needed one thing—anything—to help me survive the tidal wave of my initial lost identity two decades later, this paragraph came back to me, still fresh and still powerful and still life-giving. I think Carl Scovel kind of saved my life. I feel like his words saved my ministry, allowed my faith to endure and to deepen, even in the hardest times.

Since the introduction to this powerful paragraph, I have endured much, and I have gained even more. I am now a full-time Staff Chaplain at a hospital in Colorado Springs. And what guides me every day as I confront tragedy, tears, resilience, and hope is the idea that every person I encounter holds a goodness, a purposeful goodness, at the very core of their being too.

 Prayer

Sing in me a new song O God.
I am your singer, for a time,
and I'll live the song you want to sing
through me.

And if I can hear the song,
and be the song,
the lyrics
and the melody
all praise to you,
loving music maker.

Write in me a new story O God
a story of love and compassion
for all of life
for all people
and all creatures
and all of Your creation.

I am going to sing a new song
You say.
This is not the end of the story
You say.

Let me remember this.
Now and always.

Do a new thing
for me O God
if I am stuck in my ways
break me out of my complacency

break me out of my stubbornness
break me out of my pride
and blindness.
Do a new thing for me.

Do something new *through* me
though I am an old dog with old tricks
I want to be an old dog with new tricks
teach me, O God.
I'm listening.

I don't necessarily know what to do
make me an instrument of your peace.
I don't necessarily know how to be
make me a vessel for your grace.

Amen.

Reflection Questions

Let's look at the word *surmise*. Simply put, it's a supposition of something as true, even though there is no evidence to support it. What surmise have you had? What is your Great Surmise?

What do you think is at the heart of all creation?

What is the supreme reality of your life?

When you've been disoriented, confused, uncertain, has a passage or a mantra helped you? If so, what was it and how did it come to you?

The Temple and the Bell

*S*uppose a nun is working in the garden and hears the telephone ring. *The first thing she does is stop watering the vegetables and then she practices breathing in and out. Breathing in, "I calm myself," breathing out, "I smile." And she does that at least three times before putting down the hose and going into the office to answer the phone. Thich Nhat Hanh.*

Somewhere there is a temple,
Buddhist or Christian,
on a hillside
overlooking the persistent
crashing ocean waves.

And in that temple is a bell.
It rings before the morning prayer.
It rings before vespers.

The monks put away their brooms,
The nuns file away their papers.
They make their way to the chapel
to chant and to pray.
The sound of the bell
is the breaking through of eternity
in the everyday chores of life.

The sound of the bell
has lived on this hillside
for generations,
during the floods,
and when food was scarce,
and when the wars came.

The bell knows its work.

To signal the coming of the next thing.
To call the ones gathered to mindfulness.
To remind each one of their beat and beating heart.
To sing a song of hope and remembrance and gratitude.
To bring them back to their deepest selves.

You are the temple and the bell,
you help me to see the way home.

Prayer

This day,
This week,
This month,
O ground of our being,

teach us to listen
for the bell
that signals us to life

that calls us
from that ancient source

teach us to look for the temple
in the trees and the rising sun
the eyes of our dog, the walk of the cat.

Teach us to long
for the taste of eternity
breaking into our mundane lives,
the taste of it, the smell of it,
the sight of it, the touch of it,
the sound of it.
It is all holy and we are invited in.

Amen.

Reflection Questions

Where do you find the ringing of the bell that calls you from the deep?

Is there a sacred space that you return to again and again? What is that and what makes it special?

What is your special song of remembrance and hope and gratitude?

The Kitchen Table

Fear not, for I am with you; be not dismayed, for I am your God; I will strengthen you, I will help you, I will uphold you with my righteous right hand. Isaiah 41:10

It was January, 1956 in Montgomery, Alabama. The Montgomery Bus Boycott was a month or two old. A young minister named Martin Luther King, Jr., charismatic and strategic, emerged as a shining star in the movement.

The boycott was working. The economic impact was being felt. And that is when things started getting both serious and dangerous. King and others had assumed that the boycott would only last a few days, at most a few weeks. But it was dragging on.

King was getting so many death threats and threatening phone calls that he began to wonder if he could remain in the struggle. At one point, while in police custody, King feared that he would be lynched.

One night in particular stands out. One night turned everything around. On January 27, King had been hard at work, organizing, encouraging, and cajoling in the name of justice. All his efforts, coming from a place of non-violence.

After a long day, King returned home late at night. Coretta Scott King, his beloved wife, was asleep in the bedroom with ten-week-old Yolanda beside her.

King paced, contemplating the state of affairs. Suddenly the phone rang, breaking him from his concerns. Another death threat. "If you have no wish to die, get out of here. Leave."

It is a painful scene.

When we celebrate his birthday, we do not think of what he endured; only his speeches, his interfaith relationships, and his deep commitment to human rights. We study and celebrate his energy and his vision.

But on this night, in Montgomery, he was a young man of 27, wavering and vulnerable . . . Imagine. Think of what you experienced at 27. Consider who you were at 27. Just imagine his position.

He made a pot of coffee. He sat down at his kitchen table. Here is how he describes it:

I was ready to give up. With my cup of coffee sitting untouched before me, I tried to think of a way to move out of the picture without appearing a coward. In this state of exhaustion, when my courage had all but gone, I decided to take my problem to God. With my head in my hands, I bowed over the kitchen table and prayed aloud.

The words I spoke to God that midnight are still vivid in my memory. "I am here taking a stand for what I believe is right. But now I am afraid. The people are looking to me for leadership, and if I stand before them without strength and courage, they too will falter. I am at the end of my powers. I have nothing left. I've come to the point where I can't face it alone."

At that moment, I experienced the presence of the Divine as I had never experienced God before. It seemed as though I could hear the quiet assurance of an inner voice saying: "Stand up for justice, stand up for truth; and God will be at your side forever." Almost at once my fears began to go. My uncertainty disappeared. I was ready to face anything" (King 1958).

This epiphany comes right as Dr. King might have given up all hope. He had many options for his life path. He had his family to protect. He could easily go back to Ebenezer Baptist and live a really good life, or even teach at almost any seminary he'd like. But at the kitchen table God spoke to King and told him to keep on. A quiet assurance via an inner voice. And the fear at once began to go.

A few days later, his house was bombed. He says the kitchen table conversation with God helped him to confront it with calm and courage.

Prayer

I long for you, God,
like the deer longs for the stream,
like the deer longs for my freshly planted garden plants.

I am not the majestic lion, lord of all he surveys,
basking in the sun, calm and mighty.
I am the deer bounding across the road,
causing all the hurried humans to stop,
Hoping to not get hit, crossing anyway.
And yet, you love me.

Thank you for the love.
Thank you for the grace.
Thank you for the lion that I am not
and the deer that I am.
Thanks for the humans I impact
who will stop anyway and let me go my way,
even though I've inconvenienced them.

Thanks for the road and the garden
and the stream.

I need your grace, O God, and your love too,
like the garden plant needs the sun
and the rain and the muddy ground.

How often I've been stuck in that mud,
and how often you've whispered in my ear:

> *I'm right here. We've got this.*
> *Get up. All is well.*
> *All is well. All will be well.*

Amen.

Reflection Questions

King was guided through and through by a sense of non-violence, his first principle. Above all, what is your first principle?

God's voice here is an inner voice, quiet, and assuring. How do you hear the Divine? Describe a time when you've had such an experience.

What is your dream?

Gladys Hitchings and the Blessing

Be grateful for whatever comes because each has been sent as a guide from beyond. Rumi, The Guest House, lines 15–17

I served a Davenport church from 2002-2009. In the early years of my ministry, Gladys would come to church twice a year, when her now-mid-70s "kids" came to town.

Both visits each year, she sat in the same place, close to the windows.

I knew Gladys from the time she was 100 until she died at 103, as I recall. When I first met her, she was living with peers in an old Victorian home. It had lots of trees and a river close by. Inside, she was watching C-Span with headphones on, talking to the politicians on the screen, nibbling the bounty of muffins on the counters.

After each service she attended, her daughter would bring Gladys in her wheelchair over to me at the receiving line. Gladys would grab my hands, a big smile on her face, a twinkle in her eyes. "I'm *so* glad you're here," she'd say.

She didn't read what I wrote, I'm sure. I doubt she could even hear my sermons. But, out of a deep place of gratitude and generosity, she'd bless me, whether I deserved it or not.

Prayer

I'm seeing a lot of pain. A lot of suffering. A lot of righteous indignation. Justifiably. We are in a tough time. And I don't know what to say. Or do. I will do my little part to say, over and over, to stand up for human dignity and human rights.

And I keep coming back and back to the poetic utterances: God looked at the diversity of all things and said it is good. it is very good.

I have nothing to say. But I'll offer this prayer. For the broken and the broken hearted and the suffering and the hurting. One love. One family. One world.

Maybe tonight you are not 100 percent.

Maybe just now you are hurting,
or struggling,
or in pain.

Maybe you are distracted or confused.

Just a reminder that God,
when looking upon all of God's creation,
even you, even me, said, *It is good*
and it is beautiful.

So, rest this evening, knowing you are precious
in God's sight and that you are enough.

You are a good gift.

O God, we give you thanks for all of your creation,

all of your people. Comfort the sick and the hurting,
the ones who are easy to ignore,
whose voices are silenced
and who have no access to the gates of power.

Give strength to the weak,
give courage to the fearful,
give wisdom to the confused.

And bless all with peace.

Amen.

Reflection Questions

Gladys said: I'm so glad you're here. Name those for whom you are grateful. If they are of blessed memory, write them a letter. If they are alive, share with them why you are grateful for them. Be specific.

How do you express your appreciation to those in your life?

What's in Your Bible?

Let all guests who arrive be received like Christ, for He is going to say, "I came as a guest, and you received Me" And to all let due honor be shown. The Rule of St. Benedict

Once, a number of years ago while living in Davenport, I officiated at a wedding in Captiva Island, Florida.

At the rehearsal dinner, I sat with Reverend Dr. John Hall, former Dean of the Trinity Cathedral in Davenport and his wife Kay. I spent some time that weekend with John, hearing about his life in ministry.

John recounted a story that stuck with him over the years. It went something like this:

One day, a young Evangelical decided to come to the Unitarian Church in Davenport, with a Bible in hand. She looked around and saw that only she carried it. Perplexed, she leaned in towards someone close by asking, "Where are the Bibles?"

The response was that it wasn't really part of the culture.

"But do you believe in the Bible?"

The person responded, "We believe in many Bibles!"

John chuckled recounting the story. What a wonderful, perfect response! We do indeed believe in many Bibles! The sun in its sky; the water as our witness. We believe in lots of places to find inspiration. We believe that revelation hits us from sources near and wide, both expected and unexpected. John got a great deal of enjoyment out of telling that story.

I love that story too. (By the way, the young woman found a church that was a better fit.)

What or who is in your Bible?

In mine: James Baldwin? Check! Toni Morrison? Check! Garcia Marquez, Billy Collins? I say yes! Milocz? Yes! Mary Oliver, Annie Dillard? Why not! All kinds of folks make the list. The Book of Job? The Book of Ecclesiastes? Yes! The passage on love from Corinthians? The Sermon on the Mount? Yes, Yes. Julian of Norwich. Theresa of Avila. All, all of Thomas Merton.

The question becomes: How shall one decide what is worthy of our deepest attention, worthy of our deepest reflection? What would you put in the holy scripture of your life? What is essential to your way of thinking, believing, being, and acting? What makes the grade? Why? What has shifted over time for you?

Where do you go for wisdom? Do you take a hike? Do you study the Bible? Perhaps you pray or talk to friends, family, or your partner. Maybe you turn to your therapist, your own mentor, or maybe you just go within. Where do you go, and how do you figure out what to do?

Of course, the Bible you create is the very stuff of your life. God speaks through us and to us in the everyday, the ups and downs, the losses and triumphs, the silence, the tears, the hand shaking towards the sky. In our own little world, we too are Job, Paul on the way to Damascus, Rachel crying, Ezekiel and Amos.

Prayer

God,

Help us to see a sacred text in every person we encounter today.

Help us to see in our own face in our own body a sacred text.

Help us to see the holy, divine, shining holy of holies in our mundane, sacred every day.

Fill us, then, with wonder and amazement.

Fill us, then, with new eyes to see.

Birth in us a sense of the holy, the divine, in all of it.

Find our hearts and our eyes open so we might know where to find You,
in every person and in all things.

Amen.

Reflection Questions

Where do you go for wisdom? Do you take a hike? Study the Bible? Maybe you pray or talk to friends or your sister or your partner. Do you ask your therapist? Do you simply think on it? Where do you go and why, to figure out what to do?

What is in your bible? Who? What passages in your very own bible make you so happy?
Take some time, uninterrupted time, and build your very own bible.

Do You Love 'Em?

"Tender words we spoke to one another are sealed in the secret vaults of heaven. One day like rain, they will fall to earth and grow green all over the world." Rumi

It was either 1999 or 2000 during my time at Wesley Theological Seminary, pursuing a Masters of Divinity on my way to being ordained as a Unitarian Universalist minister.

I was studying at Wesley because I lived in D.C. many years and wanted to stay in D.C. Wesley encouraged Unitarian Universalist students to study there and Wesley was known for its progressive political and theological orientation. I loved Wesley. We were a great fit for one another.

I remember one night a few friends and I headed out to the Washington National Cathedral to hear Archbishop Desmond Tutu. We were excited. We got there early, with plenty of time to spare, so we could get a good seat.

My friends and I were all in Church History that semester. I remember distinctly that we all brought little index cards with definitions and dates and key figures so we could study and quiz each other during any extra time we might find. I remember that one professor, Ted Campbell, used to tell us that God worked through the crazy key figures in history. I liked that idea.

Even with plenty of time to spare, the place was packed.

After settling, I pulled out my index cards: Athanasius. The Cappadocian Fathers. The Council of Nicea. I began reviewing and studying my cards. As the audience awaited Desmond Tutu's place on the stage, I pondered my cards and the beautiful drama that each represented. Intrigue. Love. Spying. Compassion. Wars. Beauty. The paradox of it all. The juxtaposition of it all.

The person next to me started to laugh, an engaging, full laugh that I could tell was not mean-spirited. I looked up from my index cards and toward the woman next to me: middle aged, big smile, southern accent.

I smiled at her, as if to say, "Yes?"

She said, "I'm an Episcopal Priest. I serve a church in Southern Virginia. I am laughing because I remember learning all that stuff in seminary."

She told me that she had gone to the School of Theology at the University of the South in Sewanee.

We talked for a bit. I told her I had a test coming up the next day. She said, "Yes. You have to take that stuff. Learn it all. We all had to do that, so you do too. But once you get settled in a church, I have a little secret for you. Want to hear it?"

"Of course," I said.

She told me with a gentle wisdom, 'They don't care so much about that stuff. All they really want to know is: Do you love 'em? If you can say *Yes* to that, all the other stuff falls into place."

I can't remember one thing Desmond Tutu said (though I'm sure he was brilliant), but I've never forgotten the wisdom delivered to me through that southern Episcopalian woman, so full of laughter and wisdom.

Prayer

Then let us first of all have grace.

Grace for those who have come before us.
Sometimes they got it right, sometimes not.
But we know more now because of them.
If not grace, then gratitude.

Next let us have some grace
for each one in their own particularity.
We must always strive for common ground
and work from there.
If not grace, then an open heart.

Finally, let us have some grace
for ourselves. Knowing, we too
can be wretched, to use a big word,
or just plain old wrong, to be more direct.
If not grace, then a bit of self-compassion.

And let us, in the end, hate the parts of us
that are warlike more than we hate the other
we imagine to be. And let us say, looking
in the mirror: Have mercy on me, have mercy
on me, have mercy on me. So that we might
have mercy on all of creation.

If not mercy, then love. Above all, love.

Amen.

Reflection Questions

Who, out of the blue, gave you advice you'd never forget and what happened?

Where and how have you caught some wisdom? Describe it.

What do you remember of the wisdom your folks gave you? A teacher? A sibling?

What wisdom do you wish to pass on to your loved ones?

Buddha and Jesus and the Goddess Were Sitting Around Talking

If you desire to devote yourselves entirely to God and to be light of the children of Adam, forgive those who have done you evil, visit the sick who do not visit you, be kind to those who are unkind to you, and lend to those who do not repay you. The Muslim Jesus: Sayings and Stories in Islamic Literature, passage 65

Buddha and Jesus and the Goddess were sitting around talking.

They were talking and Jesus was expressing his concern.

"I don't know. I'm worried. The planet. The killing. I don't think they heard me when I said, 'Love your enemies. Walk towards compassion. Turn the other cheek.'"

The Buddha shook his head, "I know. I don't think they heard me say that All is One."

The Goddess said, "I probably should have been louder when I said to stay close to the earth and her rhythms in some different way. They might have heard me."

There was some melancholic silence. Jesus spoke up.

"You know I'm thinking about zapping them with a big huge love tidal wave. I mean if I can change the water to wine, I can change the hate to love, just with the wave of an arm. No one could refuse. Everyone would be compassionate and kind."

As Jesus was talking, the Spirit happened by and overheard. "No. No. That's my turf. Step back. Take a breath."

Buddha laughed and pointed at Spirit, "That's what I always say: take a breath! That's a good one."

Goddess said, "You know you can't short-circuit the process. Each has to get there on her own, on his own, on their own. Each has to find a way to bring down their walls of defensiveness, divisiveness, shame, guilt, bias, prejudice, and move towards love and unity. And some get closer than others. But if you force it, the whole gig is up."

Jesus looked at Buddha, "I never know. Is it *gig* or *jig*?" Buddha ignored him and just started dancing.

Buddha said, "The invitation is always right in front of each one to see the beauty all around."

No one had noticed that Carl Sandburg, the divine poet, had crept alongside the circle, guitar in hand. "Excuse me. Sorry to interrupt. Rumi and I were just talking about all of this the other day. And I read him my poem, 'Happiness.' Want to hear?"

Buddha, "Of course. Please."

Happiness
I ASKED the professors who teach the meaning of life to tell me what is happiness.

And I went to famous executives who boss the work of thousands of men.

They all shook their heads and gave me a smile as though I was trying to fool with them.

And then one Sunday afternoon I wandered out along
the Desplaines River
And I saw a crowd of Hungarians under the trees with
their women and children and a keg of beer and an
accordion.
(Sandburg 1950)

Prayer

Feel your breathing right now.
The inhale. The exhale.
The Holy Spirit is Breath.
The Goddess is Breath.
Life is Breath.

Calm your mind.
Sit still.
Sitting still is an act of revolutionary love.
It is an act of radical resistance.
Inhale peace. Exhale love.
All of that. Feel the earth move
under your feet. All of that.

Trust that you are right where you are supposed to be.
Trust that you know deep in your bones the next step,
the next step, the next step.

Know the power of your faith,
Whatever you call yourself or don't call yourself.
However you identify, or don't.
Let the holy, in your breathing,
Shine on to you and in to you,
The power of just being, you.
At this moment. With this breath.

Amen.

Return to your breath. How does being aware of your breath help to calm you?

Look around. What do you notice? The power of observation is a key to the kingdom. What do you notice, right in this precious moment?

Take a moment of silence. What is the silence trying to tell you?

Let's imagine you are at a dinner party with Jesus, the Goddess, the Buddha, Muhammad, and others: What would you ask them? What would you want to know?

How do you think Jesus, the Goddess, the Buddha, Muhammad, etc., would answer your questions?

What is the power of your faith?

God Say a Word

Exodus 20, the 10-commandment chapter, begins:
And God spoke all these words…
Immediately followed by words right from God's mouth!
It's so straightforward. So simple. So direct.

I'm sitting here jealous because in all of my days, God hasn't spoken to me like that. Even when I've felt enveloped in the light of God's grace and care, I have never heard with my ears, straight from God's mouth. Once, while driving out on I-95, going to see my friends for Thanksgiving dinner and the Indigo Girls were playing on the car CD, I felt such light surrounding me. It was truly mystical.

At that moment, did I feel that I was loved? Yes. I was seeing my friends that have been dear to me since I was in 3rd grade. Did the beautiful blue sky and the crisp fall air heal me? Yes. Was it the musical stylings of Amy and Emily, the Indigo Girls in all their glory? Yes.

And, it felt like more than that. It felt like being held in divine love.

But there were no *words*. No words from God. No words at all. My contemplative friends would say: Of course, there were no words. It's post-words. It's beyond words. It's ineffable.

How I long for a simple word from God! My wife, Marta, is a minister in the United Church of Christ—the ones who—mostly recently—brought us the slogan: God is still speaking.

It's true I suppose. God speaks in the trees. The aspens. The evergreens. The pines, the pines, where the sun never shines. The top of Monarch Mountain. The line where the trees just stop growing up on Pikes Peak. The sun and the moon. The face of my beloved. One Friday, there was a bird that convinced me the world made sense. Sometimes it's in the simple; other times, the profound.

Recently, I walked into a room of a patient, an elderly woman, who was about to be liberated from her intubation, a terminal wean. The family wanted a chaplain bedside and I walked in, quietly, gently. I saw God speak. A son whispering in his mother's ear. And a daughter holding her hand, weeping. And the neighbor of this patient, just like that, started singing an old song from Mexico that they all loved. *"Señor, Señor…"* it began. They all sang along. It was plaintive and sad, dolorous. I had no idea what they were singing and didn't need to. It was perfectly clear. They sang and sang.

I don't know. Maybe it is silly to want a direct, simple, straightforward word. Maybe I'll never be at the dining room table, saying, "And these are the words God said to me." Maybe God only speaks through the loving neighbor who knows the song that is just right for the occasion, the Indigo Girls, the mountain and the bird in flight. That might be enough, and likely is.

But I'll keep my heart and my ears open, just in case.

 Prayer

Listen.
Be quiet.
Be still.
Be gentle.

Relax your jaw.
Loosen your shoulders.

Listen.
Be gentle.
Be still.
Be quiet.

Let the silence
and the stillness
make sacred
the place
you're in
right now.

Look at the light
or the table
or the cloud
or the moon
or the sun
or the
wild wind through
the wild trees.

They too are a sacred text.

Listen.
Be still.
Be gentle.
Be quiet.

The world does not need your words.
Let your mind crawl into your heart space
and let it take a nap for a little while.

There's nothing to think.
There's nothing to know.

Surrender to that silence.

Let a still quiet gently keep you
just for a while.

Amen.

Reflection Questions

What is your relationship to silence?

What is a way you "hear" God?

Have you ever been going along and had an epiphany, a revelation, like during my trip out to the suburbs, listening to the Indigo Girls?

What do you think of that very religious, very spiritual word *surrender*?

Whose silence are you?

A Chaplain's Reflections from the Frontline: COVID-19

He will say: "O, son of Adam, I was hungry and you forgot to feed me." And the answer will come: "How could I feed you? You are the Lord of the worlds?" The response will come: "Did you not hear when my servant so and so, the daughter of so and so felt hunger?" Muhammad, Hadith 18

As a chaplain, my first COVID-19 death was April of 2020. He was the second person in my county to die of this vilified virus. He had been at our hospital's ICU for a week or so, going downhill quickly.

When I first saw him, on a late Wednesday night, he was upside down, to help take the weight out of his lungs, in a final effort to keep him alive. The mystery of this virus keeps everyone guessing.

I was called in around 10 p.m. to support the family. COVID-19 was new then, and no one knew what to make of it. The family of this man, healthy until all of this, was convinced that somehow medical technology and know-how could save his life.

Because of protocols handed down by national, state, and county officials, our hospital had established a no-visit policy unless a person was dying. For days, only his wife had been able to be with him, but tonight, she was joined by their two sons. They were heavily masked and garbed for viral protection, and he remained face-down in an effort to prolong his life.

As I arrived, the wife was going in to see her beloved. I witnessed the nurse lovingly put a gown on the wife, tied it in the back. Gently, she put a PAPR on her, making sure it was secure so the wife would not get this awful disease. Everyone, everyone knew this would be the last time the woman would see her husband alive. The two sons put on their personal protective equipment and joined their mom and dad in his room.

For three hours they stood there—talking to him, sharing stories, telling him he was loved beyond measure. At 1 a.m., I saw the same nurse quietly take off the wife's gown and PAPR, and assist their sons from their garb. Another COVID death. Another statistic in this infuriatingly contagious and unpredictable pandemic.

People ask me, "Roger, where do you see God in all of this COVID madness?"

I saw God, in the form of a nurse, lovingly tending to a wife seeing her husband for the last time. A wife in shock and denial and grief and overcome by it all, overwhelmed.

And I saw God hug the woman, once the man had been turned over and liberated from this wild, unexpected world.

I saw God in the care and tenderness of sons to their mother, in a wife to her husband, in a family together at the end of a life.

I saw God so many times that night.

I saw God because I was looking.

When the woman came out at 1 a.m., her husband now dead, bookended by her two sons, she looked at me and asked, "What more should I have done?" Silence. "What do we do now?"

Prayer

Give rest to the weary, O God.

Give humility to the arrogant.

Give comfort to the afflicted.

Give healing to the sick.

Give peace to the troubled.

Give awareness to all of us
that we might become filled with love and compassion.

We pray in faith and in hope and in love.

Amen.

Reflection Questions

What is your image of God during this pandemic?

If someone asked, where are you seeing God in this time, what would
you say?

How are you engaging in self-care?

49

The Death of the Buddha

Let us not become weary in doing good, for at the proper time we will reap a harvest if we do not give up. Galatians 6:9

We know that the Buddha's mother had a dream. A white elephant offered her a flower and entered her side and ten months later the baby was born. That baby who would become the Buddha.

We know that it was prophesied that this baby would become a great ruler or some kind of holy man.

We know that he was born to some pretty big privilege. And that above all, he was raised to not have to experience or even encounter any of the normal suffering that comes along with living a human life.

And we know that somehow, at some time, he was taken beyond the gates of his sheltered growing up place. And that on his ride, he came face to face with a sick man, a corpse, and an old, old man. "What is this?"

His driver told him the truth: "This is what happens to everyone. This is what it means to be alive."

And we know that he had to go out on a quest, to learn for himself what it meant to be fully human.

After a few false starts, he became enlightened. He became a teacher. He became a guide. He became the Buddha. No easy journey. But he found his way. He found his tree. He found his path.

And he discovered that all creation is endowed with all of the keys to fulfillment and happiness, but unhappiness prevails because we just aren't aware of the possibilities.

But what I'm drawn to is his death. What fascinates me are those last moments. Maybe he ate some bad pork or maybe some bad mushrooms. I don't know. He was 80 years old. He asked to be laid on his side, as his students and friends wept.

"It is okay," he said. "It is a beautiful, amazing world. I would gladly bask in this beautiful world for another 100 years. But the time has come. It is okay."

It is said that when he died, the earth shook. The trees bloomed and the petals of this new life fell gently on his body. I like to think this is precisely what happened.

Before he died, he said: *Be your own light.*

"I can die happily. I have not kept a single teaching hidden in a closed hand. Everything that is useful for you, I have already given. Be your own guiding light. Everything is impermanent. Strive, and do so diligently," the Buddha said.

Prayer

May life surprise you today.
May a sense of grace come out of nowhere in the middle
of your daily tasks.
May a sense of peace find you
in the unlikeliest of places.
May a sense of courage and renewal find you.
May God's love surround you.
And may a gentleness, a returning quietness,
and a restoring stillness be with you,
now and always.
A restorative wholeness is yours to claim and embrace.
And may faith, hope, and love be your constant companions.
God bless your day.
Amen.

Reflection Questions

When did you come in contact with suffering? What has it taught you?

How do you understand yourself as a light in the world? How do you attempt to make of yourself a light?

What false starts were part of your journey and why are they important? What did you learn from them?

A Deep Dive

WRITE YOUR ODYSSEY

When I was in parish ministry full-time, I periodically went to gatherings with clergy. Unitarian Universalist ministers do a good job of gathering regularly to retreat together, talk together, get to know one another, and to support each other.

During those times, one regular, ongoing event was the Odyssey. The most senior minister, who had not already given an Odyssey, was invited to spend an hour sharing their spiritual journey. It was normally after dinner, on a Saturday evening. Drinks were free and flowing.

An odyssey in this regard is the telling of a story of one's own life that follows the pattern of Odysseus who had to go on a journey to find his way home.

The minister who spoke owned the floor. Any format. Lecture or interactive. They could share slides. They could hand out poems. They could speak the whole hour, or speak part of it, and engage conversation.

Those Odysseys stick with me more than any other part of those retreats. (Well, once John Dominic Crosson joined us in rural Minnesota and started his workshop with, "So now I know where the end of the world is." That too was memorable.)

Everyone should gather friends. Buy some wine. And share their odyssey. Yes, even you introverts. Even you atheists and humanists and ex-this and recovering-thats. All of us.

There is no right way to do one of course. But you might include some key ideas.

1) Where did you come from and how did the land and the geography teach you something about life? As Mr. Rogers asked the journalist, who among those in your life "loved you into being"?

2) What questions animated your childhood? What were you taught about the religious life, or the spiritual life, if anything? What sayings stick with you?

3) When you went on a quest for understanding, perhaps in college, what did that look like? I visited Episcopal Churches, Quaker meetings, and UU congregations. I talked to United Methodist ministers and friends. I tried lots of different things. What have you tried?

4) Who mentored you, once you found your new wine in your old wineskin? Who taught you and helped you and let you know where to look as opposed to what to find?

5) What did loss and grief teach you?

6) What lapses occurred and how and why and what did you learn?

7) In the midst of those lapses, in the midst of the lost moments, what kept you afloat? How?

8) Where are you now and what is emerging anew?

9) How did you change your mind?

10) What practices have you tried on? Cast aside? Kept? What practices endure?

11) What gifts do you in particular bring to the world? What are your particular talents?

12) What causes your soul to come to life?

And, put it all in a story. And share. Share with your friends, your neighbors, your family.

Why share? To remind yourself that you are not alone.

For Ash Wednesday
(or I'm alive, for now, so I think I'll live)

Therefore, since we are surrounded by so great a cloud of witnesses, let us also lay aside every weight and sin which clings so closely, and let us run with perseverance the race that is set before us. Hebrews 12:1

"In a world that is full of plastic smiles and cheap grace, ashes come as a kind of relief."

Clarke Wells

Here I need not pretend.

Here I need not put on a brave face.

Here I can say: this is my heart, tattered, and torn asunder.

And here is my courage, fully intact.

And here are my innermost thoughts
and here is my public face
and I've done what I can to make them one and the same.

I've failed more often than not.

So I enter into God's grace.

I enter into God's peace.

I silence my thoughts.

I welcome the quiet.

Go ahead, put the ashes on my head.

I know one day I'll be in a bed
tied up to oxygen,
my family all around.

I've decided, truly,
that for me, the suffering God can help.

The One who says: "My shoulders are heavy,
my back aches," as we walk in the exile.

Put the ashes on my head.

One day that will be me on the bed, and the doctor
will say it is time to turn off the machines that measure
blood pressure and heart rate, and just let him peacefully go.

It is ok. Today, no fake smiles. No easy answers. No cheap grace.
Just some ashes and a friendly reminder.
From ashes to ashes. One and all.

Thank you, O God. Give us occasion to remember, today and always.

Prayer

Yea. Though I work through the shadow of the valley of death,
I will fear no evil.
You are with me.
Nothing that life can throw at me can crush me.
Nothing can separate me from your love, O God.
For this and so much more, we say Thank you God.
Thank you, God. Thank you, God.
And so it is.
Amen.

Reflection Questions

Who is in your cloud of witnesses, cheering you on?

What are the practices in your own tradition that helps you remember that you are dust to dust, ashes to ashes? If there are none, what could you imagine doing to help you remember such things?

What worries you about death?

What do you think comes after death?

Hey You, Peace Be With You

Jesus came and stood among them and said, "Peace be with you." John 20:19

Just after Easter, the disciples reacted to Jesus's death and resurrection. In a profoundly human account, the disciples are locked behind closed doors, fearing for their lives—even though one of their own, Mary Magdalene, has told them that Jesus is no longer in the tomb.

We shall put aside any easy shots about men and their inability to listen to women—the truth coming through them that disrupts all conventional thinking and points to a new way, a new reality.

Instead, let's focus on the vulnerable reality of hiding behind closed doors.

> *John 20: 19. When it was evening on that day, the first day of the week, and the doors of the house where the disciples had met were locked for fear of the authorities, Jesus came and stood among them and said, "Peace be with you."*

Let me tell you a story about someone who could have stayed behind closed doors, hiding for the rest of her life, but chose to live in peace.

I went once to a RawTools event in the sanctuary of Beth-El Mennonite Church in Colorado Springs. RawTools is a group that converts guns into garden tools. A woman I had never heard of named Sharletta Evans of Aurora, Colorado was speaking.

24 years ago, Sharletta had a baby, Casson, and during that time gave her life to God. 21 years ago, Casson was killed by three teenage boys (15 and 16 years old) in a drive by shooting. In the immediate aftermath of that crime, she nearly fell apart. She felt such guilt and remorse for putting her 3-year-old Casson in harm's way. "They don't tell you that the sixth stage of grief is overwhelming guilt."

As she was telling her story inside the sanctuary, outside the church Fred Martin was blacksmithing a gun into a garden hoe, with the help of youth from a variety of churches. The image of him hammering on that gun was broadcast against the wall as Sharletta spoke. She said, "Over time, God put me in the fire and formed me into something new, into someone who could forgive those killers, just like that gun outside." It was a long time coming, and it took every bit of strength to continue on. But God said to her at some point, "Are you going to be able to forgive those boys?"

It was a question and a suggestion, she says. And she found the strength to forgive over time. She went through a restorative justice program with the now-grown men who killed her beloved son. They are truly reconciled.

Of all people, Sharletta could have stayed behind locked doors. She could have sequestered herself, and raised her surviving son. But here she is, working with restorative justice, working to reduce gang membership among young people in Colorado, telling her story, showing up and providing hope.

There are less dramatic stories, I suspect, in all of our lives. Stories that invite us to hide behind closed doors, behind locked doors, to let shame, despair, cynicism, and fear win the day. I sure identify with

those disciples. But isn't it a remarkable image of Jesus just nonchalantly walking through the locked door and saying: *Peace be with you.*

Come out into the light. The shadows are no place to live. We are
in a new world, where love overcomes hate, the light overcomes the
dark, where we can all move towards forgiveness and grace, and love
and the beauty of human dignity.

So, hey, you, lurking in the shadows, afraid to show your face,
peace be with you.

Allah, Buddha, Jesus, Mother Mary,
God, Yhwh, Sister Dorothy Day, Brother Martin,
Father Louis,

Whatever your name, whoever you call,
whoever you use,

use me,
call me.

Here I am, Lord.
Is it I, Lord.

My heart is broken.
My way is unclear.
The path is long.
My spirit is humbled.

My son is hurting.
My neighbor is crying.
The guy under the bridge, he needs a meal.
My spouse needs to be heard.

Who am I?
What can I offer?

Just this:
my broken heart that still beats,
(thank you, thank you, thank you)
my old ear that still hears,
(thank you, thank you, thank you)

my feet that have journeyed long,
that can carry me from here to there.
(thank you, thank you, thank you)

So carry me, God, however you do that,
from here to there, and I'll follow,
and I'll walk, and I'll listen,
and I'll stay awake.

Though the night is dark,
your light will guide me.

Amen.

Reflection Questions

How have you been put through the fire?

What is your take on forgiveness?

When have you wanted to hide and been assured that coming out of your hiding place is safe and okay?

When have you wanted to close off your heart but realized that having an open heart and moving into your feelings is the work of your faith journey?

This I Believe

I believe in jazz.
Structure and improv. Call and response.
I believe in healing.

I have seen it so often—among many I've known, among strangers, in my own life.

I believe in story. Once upon a time.

I believe everything you ever needed to know could be found in a parable.

I believe with the psalmists that we—you and I and all of us—can know the beauty of the lord in the land of the living.

I believe in dreams. I believe in dreamers.

I believe in something bigger than me, call it god if you'd like. I will. I believe in a god the name of which is many and never to be known but one that I call love, love that will never let us go. Fellow sufferer who understands. Holy Spirit. Spirit of Life. The inner voice of wisdom. The still, small voice. The center who listens and knows. The god found in the creative moment, the One who calls us to our best self.

I believe, more than anything, in people. People who grow. People who snore. People who curse. People who build and give. People who fail. People who love, and love again. People who know wisdom, occasionally.

I believe in the Chesapeake Bay. And the sea. I believe in the rising sun. And my children's smiles. And I believe in you, in thou. In life.

I believe that anyone at any time can know the holy way, the good way in life. That each life is holy for its own sake. We are what we've got, and I believe that we have more power and beauty and love and compassion than we realize.

Take a moment and write your own This I Believe statement. Want some help? Go to https://www.npr.org/series/4538138/this-i-believe

The Healing of Naaman

Now Naaman was commander of the army of the king of Aram. He was a great man in the sight of his master and highly regarded, because through him the Lord had given victory to Aram. He was a valiant soldier, but he had leprosy. 2 Kings 5

In early March of 1965, a group of civil rights marchers were blocked at the Edmund Pettis Bridge in Selma, on their way from Montgomery. One hundred forty marchers were injured. Reverend Dr. Martin Luther King immediately called for a second march, challenging clergy, religious leaders, and people of faith to come to Selma.

Henri Nouwen was a Dutch priest who happened to be studying in Topeka, Kansas at the Menninger Clinic. He heard the call from King but ignored it. Soon, however, a fierce, unshakeable sense came to him. *Why are you in Kansas? Why aren't you going down to Selma to march? You believe in equality. You believe this is a faith issue.*

He told his friends and they thought he was crazy. "You're just bored. You are just looking for an adventure," they told him.

But the question kept after him: *Which side are you on? Why aren't you in Selma?*

One Sunday night, even though the march had already started, he tossed and turned and finally decided. Nouwen was going to Selma.

He got out of bed with courage and determination replacing the restlessness and uncertainty of yesterday.

In Vicksburg, Nouwen came upon a hitchhiker, a young Black man standing well off the road. Nouwen stopped. It turns out Charlie was also headed to Selma. "I prayed and prayed," Charlie told Nouwen. I am putting my life in my hands, but you are my very own angel.

Charlie told Nouwen about what it was like to live as a Black activist in Mississippi and how he and his friends alternated between rage and fear balanced by determination and faith. He told Nouwen about the murder of Medgar Evers, his friend.

On and on, the stories continued. Nouwen said something interesting and profound: *Charlie was turning me into a Black man. My innocence was replaced with fear. Here I was with a Black man. My license plates betrayed me as headed to Selma to the march.*

He felt vulnerability and fear. No matter how much he tried to talk himself out of it, he was afraid. And it was his fear and his vulnerability, along with his open heart as he listened to Charlie, that lead him to this insight:

> *The fear gave me new eyes, new ears, and a new mouth.*

They made it to Selma. They were worried about a trooper that followed them. They were refused service at a restaurant. But they made it. The limits on the number of marchers meant that Charlie and Nouwen stayed at Brown's Chapel in Selma. Upon their arrival, a pair of 12-year-olds asked who they were and where they were from, as part of the organizing of the event.

The whole thing didn't appear to be terribly organized. It felt a bit chaotic. But the spirit was there. And the songs. And the prayers. And food. Somehow everyone got fed. There was always enough food.

He called the assembled "God's fools." They were idealists, pacifists, hippies, wanderers, melancholy drifters, and deep-eyed dreamers.

God's fools for love.

They had shown up. Nouwen had shown up. He encountered Charlie. The world changed in those years. And Nouwen carried this experience with him all of his life and he shared it widely.

Prayer

A Prayer for the Time of Jubilee

God of many names,
God who looked upon the diversity of the world
from the very beginning
and called it good, very good,
and beautiful, very beautiful,

Bless this time.
Bless all who have ears to hear.

We shall walk together,
this year, every year,
in truth and righteousness,
in power and light
and love.

Give us strength to walk
towards justice for all,
give us a spirit of resilience
and hope,
as we proclaim that all people
in all places
have a place at the table,
that all God's people
have a voice in the choir.

Deliver us from
this violence that has poisoned us
and lift us towards a spirit of peace.

Deliver us from tyranny,
Tyranny in our politics
Tyranny in our spirit
so that we might all be free
now and always.
Liberate us.
Bring down the haughty
and the garish and the greedy and the grim
that a spirit of joy and abundance
might claim us.

We proclaim that the captives are free
and a new world is coming, a new day is dawning.

In your many names we pray,
but mostly we pray in love and commitment
And fierce loyalty to the freeing of all souls,
then and now and always,
Amen.

Reflection Questions

When have you felt powerless, voiceless, invisible?

When have you had to listen to someone you didn't think you needed to listen to and yet learned something important?

What do you need in order to move towards liberation and freedom?

When has a calling or a question kept gnawing at you fiercely? For Nouwen, it was why he wasn't in Selma. Have you had such a question, such a calling in your life, on your journey? If so, what was that like, and how did it turn out?

Who is your Charlie? Whom did you encounter that gave you new eyes, new ears, or a new heart? For me, it was in college. My roommate at Appalachian, a gay man, opened my eyes began to see how all my stereotypes and all my religious baggage was simply wrong. I was a new person. Who was, or is, your Charlie?

What is the end you seek?

What is the vision that calls you, in the night?

Who are you going to pick up and take with you?

Who is your tribe? Who are your people who show up, no matter what? Who will feed you in the struggle, who will laugh and pray, and sing and dance with you?

Spring!

Why do you look for the living among the dead? The Gospel of Luke 24:1-12

S pring is a very special time in the life of the church, with the promise of renewal and the coming of hope, and birth of something new. Easter and Pentecost.

Easter obviously points to the reality that Jesus proclaimed is not going to be stopped by his execution; that love is bigger than that. The kingdom of God, which is based on compassion, equality, beauty, and goodness, could not be overcome by the simple matter of his death. And so it is with all of us, right? We think, *Well, the loss of that job, the ending of that relationship, the death of my beloved, I do not know how I can go on. There is no life for me left,* but something about the beauty of the resilient spirit within, will not be denied. We resurrect, we transform, we once again get back on the horse and ride. The horse is named hope, love, and faith.

Have you ever thought: *I have finally gotten so old that I shall just give in to cynicism and despair, and live out my days as a curmudgeonly, sour, old man with nothing much to offer the world, except the old familiar refrain, "Well back in my day, things were different"*?

But somehow, with the coming of spring, and just like the birth of the Buddha, or the Passover, or Easter and resurrection and Pentecost, we *are* born anew. Every day, the goal is to be born anew. Several times a day!

I heard the most remarkable tribute about someone: *He found grace high and low in this troubled world.*

What a remarkable tribute, and what a great thing to aspire to: to be a resurrection people, a people based in hope, to be someone about whom another would say that he looked for and found grace in the craziest places, high and low. Not only did he find it, but also it proved to be a sign of hope and love and peace in this broken, crazy world.

We all have resurrection stories. We have all found grace. We have all gotten back on the horse named Hope.

Consider the situation after the death of Jesus. The disciples were in a dilemma even with the empty tomb: Do we proceed? Do we keep alive the message our teacher has given us? Or shall we go back to being fishers of fish, tax collectors, farmers, and the like? With these hard questions, something urged them to keep going. The idea that despite it all, they simply kept going. And this keeping-on gives me strength and urges me also to keep going as something new is just around the corner.

Jesus appeared in some kind of form to the disciples between that period of Easter and Pentecost. And he was teaching them. He said that there is a holy spirit that would come to them. That they would not be alone. That they would *know* that they have great power.

So, Jesus went on and on about the spirit, but all they wanted to know is this: *Is this the time when you'll restore the kingdom?* They're really asking: *is everything going to be ok?*

And they asked it in this form: *Is this the time?*

And Jesus said something like this: *What do you know about the time? There is no knowing the time. The time is what it is. Focus instead on your power in the spirit, which is now, and now, and now, and now.*

There is no time but now, and the time for you being alive in the spirit and knowing you are alive in the spirit is now. Now.

Look to that. Put your gaze there. The time is now and you are stronger than you think.

And this is the best part of the story: After Jesus tells them this, he ascends into heaven.

And there is a great scene that happens.

Jesus (again) is gone. And the disciples were gazing up to heaven.

Two figures—let's call them Moses and Elijah, just for fun—came and said, "What are you looking at? Why are you gazing up there? Did your teacher not just tell you that the spirit would be with you? You gaze up there, but look inside. The answers are there. There is no *out there*, when you're talking about the life of the spirit. There's no gazing up into heaven, sitting around waiting for enlightenment. The answers are within."

In times of disruption, in times of uncertainty, in times of change, we are always tempted to say: *Well, is now the time?* This story reminds us that we can't always know the time. It reminds us that in the power of the spirit, *now* is the time to do what we can do. And in times of change, of disruption, of uncertainty, the important thing is to focus on the power within you to claim your space in the world. Don't look outside yourself for answers! Don't gaze upon the heavens passively, waiting for something to make sense of it all. *You* are the teacher you've been looking for.

Prayer

I cling to you and your ways.
I remember you night and day O God,
as one that has delivered me
from my cynicism
from my despair
from my selfishness.

In a dry and parched land,
I long for your presence,
and your assurance,
in the same way I long for water in the desert.

Amen.

Reflection Questions

Breath. Holy Spirit. Ruah. What is your image for that spirit that Jesus is talking about?

What do you think it took for the disciples to keep going after the departure of their beloved teacher and rabbi?

What is your view of the kingdom of God?

Speaking of the Kingdom of God

"After his suffering, Jesus… appeared to them during forty days, speaking to them about the kingdom of God." - Acts of the Apostles 1:3

I love stories like these that are prominent in the spring time of year. The stories from Palm Sunday to Pentecost.

Like the one of Jesus parading into Jerusalem on his little donkey, while the powerful paraded their heavy artillery.

The disciples were hiding behind locked doors, and Jesus, risen, just casually walked through the walls. "Hey. Peace be with you."

Philip kind of wanders into the Ethiopian eunuch. Casually, he throws out a couple of questions like, "Of course, I don't quite understand. Are you going to help me out or are we just going to chill in my chariot? And are you going to baptize me or not?"

And in that moment, There's some water. There is a new path. There's some new life.

All the time, in these stories, right when you think it's gotta be over this time—It has to be the end of the story—a new way emerges. A way that you never expect to open up.

In Deuteronomy or Leviticus, or wherever, the eunuch was not really invited to be a part of God's big dinner party. He wasn't supposed to be part of the inner circle. And here, Isaiah envisions a world where the eunuch *is* gathered in, making room for the circle to get wider, bigger. And just when you think you know where the story is headed, it's turned on its side! Stories like the one with Philip just smashes down all the walls. "Of course, you're invited. Of course, you'll be baptized."

No wonder Jurgen Moltmann read this stuff and saw hope over and over and over again. There's so much hope if you are looking for it. And life is like that too.

Every day it seems, someone to the right of me, someone to the left of me, is trying to get me to cower in fear. I screw up. I think this might be the end of this or that. I think I'm not enough, or that I didn't do enough, or any number of big doubts.

I'm just going to remember that all the stories suggest that God is all in all.

And I'm not going to hide behind locked walls. I'm just going to hear the voice of the one saying: *Hey, peace be with you.*

"After his suffering, Jesus… appeared to them during forty days, speaking to them about the kingdom of God." - Acts 1:2-3

He could have done so many things. He could have spoken about so many things. He could have laid out a process improvement plan for the early church.

He could have laid out a strategy.

But what did he do? He kept talking about the kingdom of God.

And what is the kingdom of God full of? Compassion and love and forgiveness.

As theologian Mary Luti writes:

Here he is, a new creation fresh from God's morning, yet not a single new topic comes out of his mouth. He's still talking about what he talked about pre-crucifixion at the lakeshore, on the mount, in the temple precincts, at Capernaum, on the road to everywhere.

"He spoke to them of kingdom of God," of debts cleared by mercy, small things of infinite worth, mighty things reduced to dust, broken bread instead of broken bodies, tiny sparrows, counted hairs, banished demons, truth declared to tyrants, put-away swords, found sheep, found coins, found children, a hidden way inside, a buried pearl, living water, branches and vine.

Even suffused with eternal light, one foot in heaven, it's all he can think to tell them. For forty days and forever: the kingdom of God. https://www.ucc.org/daily_devotional

A Prayer of Oscar Romero

It helps, now and then, to step back and take a long view.

The Kingdom is not only beyond our efforts,
it is even beyond our vision.

We accomplish in our lifetime only a tiny fraction
of the magnificent enterprise that is God's work.

Nothing we do is complete,
which is a way of saying that the Kingdom always lies beyond us.

No statement says all that could be said.
No prayer fully expresses our faith.
No confession brings perfection.
No pastoral visit brings wholeness.
No program accomplishes the Church's mission.
No set of goals and objectives includes everything.

This is what we are about.
We plant the seeds that one day will grow.
We water seeds already planted,
knowing that they hold future promise.
We lay foundations that will need further development.
We provide yeast that produces effects far beyond our capabilities.

We cannot do everything,
and there is a sense of liberation in realizing that.
This enables us to do something,
and to do it very well.

It may be incomplete, but it is a beginning, a step along the way,
an opportunity for the Lord's grace to enter and do the rest.
We may never see the end results,
but that is the difference between the master builder and the worker.

We are workers, not master builders;
ministers, not messiahs.

We are prophets of a future that is not our own.
Amen.

(Untener 1979)

Reflection Questions

Often Martin Luther King, Jr. would refer to the Beloved Community. It was his version of the kingdom of God. When King talks about being caught up in a network of mutuality, he is referring to the Beloved Community. It wasn't some lofty dream. It was something attainable. Something real and embedded in the very heart of democracy and faith. It was all grounded in nonviolence and love. Above all, love. Working together, people could get there.

What do you make of the Beloved Community? What does it mean? How do we get there? What do you do to contribute to its formation?

What are you building that will not be complete in your lifetime?

Where do you find hope?

Keep the Bible Weird

This mystery, which is Christ within you; the hope of glory. Colossians 1:27

There is such richness, such inspiration to be found in the teachings of Jesus. Okay, I'm going to admit that the Transfiguration of Jesus is my favorite story in the Bible. I think I can relate because it's just so weird. So strange indeed.

Mark's Jesus is so *normal*. His cousin, John the Baptist, is baptizing folks while Jesus is teaching people that the kingdom is at hand. Jesus is healing, praying, teaching—all the things we've come to associate with Jesus. He's the guy we all want to hang out with, right? He's eating with sinners, fighting with the Pharisees, picking out his besties, doing things his family sees as crazy; but he doesn't care! He literally could give two cares about what anyone thinks! He's teaching parables that are hard to follow, feeding people who have nothing, and performing miracle after miracle. He's offending the orthodox—the moral guardians of the law who have no idea what he's talking about—with his teachings of grace, grace, and more grace. They proclaim: For God's sake, stop eating with sinners and prostitutes! Wash your hands! Why are you healing and blessing everybody? Don't you know who they are? They don't belong with you! You're better than that!

And all the while, Jesus is expressing that his table is open. He feeds more people, performs more miracles, and blesses everyone. Over and over.

All the normal Jesus-things.

And then, he says to his beloveds: *Look, some of you before you die, you'll experience the kingdom of God in all of its mystery and majesty and power and beauty.*

We just read along, getting into all the cool Jesus-stuff, and the 9th chapter of Mark comes on like a total shift in consciousness and Jesus takes three of his people up the mountain and all kinds of weird stuff happens: his clothes get all sparkly, a voice comes from the clouds telling them stuff, and there was a possessed child to be exorcised.

You know, Thomas Jefferson took all the weird parts out of the Bible and I totally get that. I understand the impulse. It's kinda like how the Buddha was sheltered from suffering. Sometimes we think people can be more inspired by being told all the neat and tidy stories. You want so badly for people to live out the ethical and moral directives: The Golden Rule, compassion, appreciation for diversity. You want that to be the focus so much that you push away all of the strange, unexplainable stuff. I get it.

But you know, the really odd parables, and the really weird miracles, and especially the moments like the transfiguration, those keep you on your toes.

Those turn upside down all your expectations and say: *Woohoo. Wake up. Pay attention. Life isn't a then b then c then d. Sometimes life is messy. Weird. Chaotic. Pay attention to those times too.*

Life is really weird. And in the midst of the weirdness the crazy little secret is that you are going to be okay. I am going to be okay. All will be well. All will be well. All manner of things will be well.

How awesome is it that God can speak from a cloud over your head, and speak to your friends saying things like: *Hey, this is my beloved. You are my beloved. Look at all the ways of being in the world. It is beautiful and good.*

Anyway, these odd moments like transfiguration, are like water in the desert. These unexpected weird stories are like a breath of fresh air, so shocking, yet so strange!

You know how there are those bumper stickers: *Keep Manitou Weird? Keep Austin Weird?* I want one that says *Keep the Bible Weird.*

This transfiguration is the Bible at its most glorious, wonderfully, oddest.

Jesus took three of his disciples up to the mountain.

Now we know in that culture and that time, the mountain was one of the places—along with the temple—where the human could meet God.

In modern times, I don't know where you go to meet God. I don't know where you go to commune with God. We no longer really believe that you have to go to the innermost secretive place within the temple or that you have to go up a mountaintop—though I bet some of you *have* met God in church and some of you would proclaim that you've met him hiking up a mountain or walking along the shore. We no longer have God boxed in. We no longer profess that you can only find God here or there or someplace specific. Thank God there are about a million different answers among a million different folks for the question of where to find God.

Stay weird. Find God where you find God. Go there. And live your life, while you are still alive!

Prayer

Prince of peace, Sister of all, Mother Father Parent God,
Mystery within, One beyond all,

Words fail me.
I cannot catch you, all beyond all,
I cannot see you, love within.

Let me soak in this pool of peace.
Let me swim and dance in this rushing river.

I have seen the candle flame
light up the dark night.

I have seen one stroke the hair of their beloved,
In a moment of despair, and I've seen both
sit in the silence of the truest love.

I have seen the mountain, and the wind in the trees,
and I have felt the wonder and the awe
In the face of its majestic light.

I see you there God,
alight, glowing.

Give me eyes to see
and a heart to love
and feet to dance
and a hand to share with the world
and of course the healing silence.
Now and always.

Amen.

Where have you encountered God? And what was that like?

Where is a sacred space that you retreat to during times when you pray?

How is your life weird and how is it that your sacred texts help you navigate that?

How is your weird life like a sacred text?

Hagar and the Blessing

Meanwhile, God heard the boy crying. The angel of God called from Heaven to Hagar, "What's wrong, Hagar? Don't be afraid. God has heard the boy and knows the fix he's in. Up now; go get the boy. Hold him tight. I'm going to make of him a great nation."
Genesis 21:17–18

This is a story from the book of Genesis about a woman named Hagar, who had no power, and was blessed by God anyway. In all the typical stories, Abraham and Sarah get all the attention. They are the powerful ones who birthed a whole lineage. But Hagar is lifted up too. It is a great story and it goes something like this:

What a cast of characters this one has! We have Abraham (the patriarch!), Sarah (the matriarch!), Hagar (their slave and hand-maiden!), Ishmael (the baby!) and the angel of God (the villain, the savior?), who is, for our purposes at least, a proxy for God's own self. Pretty stellar lineup, huh?

These people are real and seriously flawed. Abraham and Sarah had plenty of power yet they had their own struggles. Hagar, their slave, had no power. Nothing.

Abraham has just been told he is going to have a people that will count as many as the stars. He's been told that God will never abandon him and that the covenant they make will be forever.

And Abraham thinks something like this: Yes. I love it. Sign me up. I'm all in.

But there is an issue. Abraham has no heir. He cannot bear children. He and his wife are old.

Sarah says to Abraham: God has made me unable to have children. But I do have Hagar, the Egyptian slave girl. Maybe we could have a child through her.

It works. Hagar gets pregnant. Abraham has a child, an heir. I mean, it is all very *Handmaid's Tale*. But the baby has arrived. The baby is named Ishmael.

Are you seeing any potential issues? I mean, what could possibly go wrong, right?

Sarah freaks out. Hagar got pregnant. Now Sarah is always looking at Abraham with suspicion. Abraham tells Sarah to figure out what to do with Hagar. Abraham wants nothing to do with any of this business. Sarah is mean to Hagar. Hagar runs away.

An angel of the Lord sees her and says, "You have to go back." It is really hard for me to know how to read this. We know that Hagar is a surrogate, without rights, without a voice. A slave. A nobody. Her leaving is important to her survival. Why the heck would the angel tell her to return?

Think about that.

A few things. One, we know it reinforces the sense that Hagar is without much power. She can't even run away with her baby. She can't even escape the oppressive scene. At the end of the day, the angel is, I think, a bad guy to send her back.

Well, regardless of what Hagar was thinking or not thinking, she went back. And what do you think happened? Sarah conceived. Isaac was born. Years pass. Sarah saw Isaac and Ishmael playing in the yard. She was distressed. She didn't want Isaac playing with Ishmael. "Get 'em out of here," she says to Abraham. He is torn. He is conflicted.

But at the end of the day, he gives Hagar and Ismael a bit of lunch and sends them on their way.

They are officially exiled. To be in exile, to be cast out of one's home, to experience a state of existential homelessness is a great trauma. Hagar and Ishmael are in exile. Heartbroken. With a loaf of bread and a bit of water, she and her child wander about in the wilderness of Beersheba. The water ran out. She put Ishmael under a tree. And she went off to a safe distance just out of sight, for who can look upon the death of their child? She wept. She wailed. The boy cried. God heard the boy's weeping and an angel of the Lord said to Hagar: *Do not be afraid.*

Do not be afraid. God hears the cry of the exile, the weak, the oppressed. The crying one. God hears. God says: *We will make a great nation of this youngster, Ishmael. All will be well.* Then God opened her eyes. And she saw a well of water. She went and filled the jug Abraham had given her and she gave the boy some water. And he lived. He lived a full life and found a wife and a whole people came from his lineage. God blessed Hagar and Ismael. In their cries, God blessed them. As God had blessed the crying of Abraham and Sarah in their cries when they were without child.

Sarah just wanted her gone. Disappeared, out of sight, out of mind. God had other things in mind.

But in this story, at least as I read it, no one gets out of here without a blessing. The one you want to put into the wilderness because they annoy you, they're getting a blessing. The one you think is insensitive and mean, they're getting a blessing too. The baby, crying, lost and alone, without water, he too is getting blessed. The child, born to the old rich powerful parents, getting blessed.

So we may as well try to figure out how to look upon everyone we see, the ones with power, the ones without power, as a carrier of the divine image. The ones perpetually suffering and in exile, carriers of the divine image. The ones perpetually winning and seemingly without a care in the world, carriers of the divine image.

Everyone. Blessed.

Prayer

God of life and love and mystery,
God of one thousand names.

Too much am I Ishmael, crying in the desert.
Where is your face, if you have so many names?

Too much am I Sarah, casting off bad decisions—
Banishing inconvenience out to the desert to die.
Where is the blessing, if yours is the kingdom at hand?

Too much am I Abraham, indecisive, passive
in the face of conflict.
Where is the covenant, if the covenant is for love's sake alone?

Too much in exile, too much in Babylon,
Too much weeping in this foreign land,
And I, far from home, can't sing my holy songs.

So where is the prophet, the teacher, if finally comes
the poet singing:
"Comfort, O comfort by people?"
We wait and we wait.

Shake me up in my complacency;
I feel like going on.

Shake me up in my delirium;
I will not be moved.

Quicken in me this sense of love;
I too have a dream.

Amen.

Reflection Questions

How are you like Abraham?

How are you like Sarah?

How are you like Hagar?

How are you like Ishmael?

What does this story say to you about God?

Where is God in All of That?

Where can I go to flee from your Spirit? Psalm 139: 7

When I think about the most important questions for anyone on a spiritual journey, I think of these three questions:

Who Am I?
What Do I Want?
And Who/What is God?

Another question that I love to ponder, also from the world of spiritual direction, is "Where is God in all of that?" I've asked that many times as a chaplain.

I met recently with the family who needed a simple graveside service for their wife/mother/grandmother, named Audrey.

I sat with them at the funeral home: *Tell me about Audrey.*

The stories gushed out. Her grandson talked about how she taught him to cook and how he helped her clean the sink when he was a child. He loved cleaning the sink. Something about the Ajax and the bubbles. Until the end, they cleaned sinks together.

Another person mentioned her garden. Her sons loved gardening with her. They loved both pulling weeds and collecting the bounty she had so carefully nurtured.

Someone mentioned her pineapple upside-down cake, and someone else, her love of quilting, which turned into gifts for children in crisis, baby blankets, and so on. There was a quiet generosity to her life.

I sat there, reminded once again, that life is so much about the small moments. The sink and the pineapple upside down cakes. And the simple garden.

Where is God in all of that? So often we think it is the big things that folks will remember, the big accomplishments, the big promotions and so on. But time and again, listening to folks in the hospital or before the funeral, it is the sacred, quiet moments that endure and remain. God is in those moments. The sacred, quiet, simple things.

So, when I asked them what readings might be appropriate for her service, I was not surprised that all of them had to do with love. Her husband said that he'd found her Bible that she got at First Presbyterian Church when she was nine years old (75 years ago). All the underlined parts had to do with loving yourself, loving your neighbor, and loving God.

The making of the pineapple upside down cake, or the stuffed shells, or the carrots in your garden, they're all the ingredients of a holy sacred life. God's in the cleaning of the sink, the quilting, the being together.

Prayer

Let nothing disturb you,
Let nothing frighten you,
All things are passing away:
God never changes.
Patience obtains all things
Whoever has God lacks nothing;
God alone suffices.
Amen. (Attributed to St Theresa)

Reflection Questions

Write your obituary.

Write an ethical will for your children and their children, or your loved ones, near and far.

What memories will folks hold of you?

How do you try to pay attention to the sacred ordinary?

Dietrich Bonhoeffer and Albert Franklin Fisher: Berlin and Birmingham in New York

If you bring forth what is within you, what you bring forth will save you. The Gospel of Thomas, verse 70.

In 1930, at the age of 24, famed Lutheran pastor Dietrich Bonhoeffer came to New York City to study at Union Theological Seminary, a leading Protestant seminary in the United States, both then and now.

In New York, he was not especially impressed by Union. But what made a huge impression on him was his friendship with Albert Franklin Fisher, a Black student at Union. Fisher was from Birmingham and Bonhoeffer was from Berlin. Fisher introduced him to jazz and to Abyssinian Baptist Church, where Adam Clayton Powell, Sr. was minister. In 1930, Powell was beginning his ministry. And it did not take long for Bonhoeffer to get wrapped up in the worship and the life of that remarkable church. It was so different from the worship he was used to in Germany. He led Sunday school class and a women's Bible study. What a remarkable year he had with those folks. They welcomed him with open arms.

I remember that he wrote something like this: Here (at Abyssinian) you can really hear the Gospel. You can hear sin and grace and ultimate hope. I have learned to feel the gospel in the (Black) church.

Bonhoeffer would say that worship at Abyssinian was the only time he experienced true religion in the United States. He felt that the only folks who could properly understand the depths of worship were the marginalized community up in Harlem; that they were the ones who could really grasp the hope and liberation of the gospel of Jesus.

At Union, Professor Reinhold Niebuhr challenged him to think about how church doctrine impacted social and political life. Racism, lynching, and Jim Crow laws were big topics in the United States at that time.

It is this encounter with "the other," this encounter with Albert Fisher, that changed Bonhoeffer. If he had stayed in his Union cocoon and never visited Abyssinian, he would have never truly felt worship in a way he said he never felt in the German intellectual Lutheranism of his home.

He never would have felt deep in his bones the liberating message of Abyssinian Baptist and Adam Clayton Powell. He would never have learned that the gospel has a word of liberation and radical equality to say in the here and now, and not just in the great hereafter.

So, after his year in New York, he returned to Germany. After his epiphanies at Abyssinian, Bonhoeffer took them back to Germany and applied them to his own context which revolved around anti-Semitism, another dehumanizing impulse. When German Protestant churches fell in line with the National Socialists, he and others founded the confessing church, as part of the resistance. He founded an underground seminary, Finkenwalde. And, he joined a group that aimed to assassinate Hitler. It failed and Bonhoeffer was executed in Spring 1945, a few weeks before the end of World War II.

Something happened to Bonhoeffer in Harlem. What happened was that in the real encounter with difference, with *the other*, he opened his mind and his heart. His theology, which was rich and deep even as a young man, traveled from his head to his heart. He *felt* God's love. He felt liberation. And he wanted to be a part of the humanizing of his faith, in the direction of liberation and radical equality. He wanted a faith that recognized and celebrated the full humanity of each person, the full dignity. He wrote, "The individual belongs essentially and absolutely with the other, according to the will of God, even though, or even because, each is completely separate from the other" (Bonhoeffer 1951).

One time, Fisher and Bonhoeffer went down to D.C. to visit the Federal Council of Churches and to visit Fisher's alma mater, Howard University. While there, they were refused service in a restaurant. They left, but the discrimination and the hatred surely impacted Bonhoeffer forever.

It is after all, Bonhoeffer (1951) who wrote during his imprisonment:

There remains an experience of incomparable value. We have learned for once to see the great events of world history from below, from the perspective of the outcast, the suspects, the maltreated, the powerless, the oppressed, the reviled—in short, from the perspective of those who suffer…The perspective from below must not become the partisan expression of those who are eternally dissatisfied; rather we must do justice to life in all its dimensions from a higher satisfaction, whose foundation is beyond any talk of "from below" or "from above."

My teacher, Josiah Ulysses Young, III, wrote, "Bonhoeffer takes us to the heart—and thus to the truth—of what is at stake in a Christian's life of faith. And what is at stake is whether we can live in this world, without illusion, and with a no-holds-barred commitment to one another—for Christ's sake" (Bonhoeffer 1998).

Prayer

Way-maker when there seems to be no way,
Way-shower,
Friend of the poor and oppressed,

Grant us peace.
Deliver us from our prejudices and our biases.
Well, at least help us out when we try to take the next step towards
anti-racism.
It is our journey to take. You walk alongside.

Help us to dream the beloved community,
to visualize and imagine it.
Help us to do our little part to help bring it forth,
on earth as it is in heaven.

Help us to encounter those who are different
and see your face, your love, your image.

Amen. May it be so.

Reflection Questions

There is a marvelous picture of Bonhoeffer with his students at Finkenwalde. They are listening to a phonograph of American Black spirituals. What role does religious music play in your faith? Have you listened, for instance, to Mahalia Jackson singing "How I Got Over"? There are over 4.5 million views on YouTube. Check it out. Or have you heard Marian Anderson sing "Ave Maria"? Or The Detroit Mass Choir sing "The Storm is Passing Over"? What about other types of music? What does that do for your spirit?

Bonhoeffer has a very this-worldly theology. What does it mean to live in a world where we don't need the idea of God as a hypothesis to resolve most issues related to science and everyday life?

Reflect on the long quotation above and about seeing the world from the point of view of the tortured, the exiled, the oppressed, the hated. Take some time absorbing this text. What does it say to you?

Psalm 1: A Riff

Look. The ones who tend their garden
And find the love of the holy one in their own way
And who bend their ear towards the sacred stillness

They will walk the path ahead of them
With purpose and peace,
Dwelling not in the place of anxious busyness.

Sacred Silence will be their forever friend.
They will know now and always that they belong.
And will welcome friends and strangers alike
To their table of abundance.

They'll be like the tree that you
See from your window
The one down by the creek
That bears fruit in season
Every single year.

Prayer

We Sing Your Praises
O God, we sing your praises.
Even when the day is long.
Even when the path is unclear.
Even when we are scattered and divided. We sing your praises.

For the gift of this day.
For another chance to seek reconciliation and unity.

For the gift of family and friends. For our tribes.
For the opportunity to learn new things.
Ground us, O God, in gratitude.
We sing your praises.
Amen.

Reflection Questions

The Psalms give us permission to cry out, rejoice, lament, find our way.

How have you found consolation in the Psalms?

What is your favorite Psalm?

Take on a project: Pick a favorite Psalm and write it in your own voice and with your own images.

Belief and Belonging

*Belief brings me only to your door. I must disappear
into your mystery before I can come in. Hakim Sanai,
Sufi*

A terrorism expert spoke about a 1983 bombing of the US
Capitol, something I had never heard of before even though
I spent the first four years of my career working in the Hart
Senate Office Building. He said that because we believe domestic
terrorism is rare and fleeting, we tend to forget about the instances
quickly.

The group that bombed the Capitol was named N19, a group of
women (and a couple of men) who railed against imperialism.

The terrorism expert went on to talk about how they were true
believers. Their ideology was front and center. They were committed.
He said white supremacists and other domestic terrorists also have
this ideology: driven, true-believer status.

He said, "It all boils down to belief and belonging."

I stopped in my tracks.

So much of my religious belief, growing up, was centered on the
idea that some people win and some lose. And the ones who won
looked like us, acted like us, thought like us, believed like us, talked
like us, and so forth. And so much of what I believed was that those
who thought differently would end up in hell and it was our job to

save them from hell. In retrospect, it was all incredibly immature and stupid.

And then, once I decided on a different course, it took me a long, *long, LONG* time to get to a place where I didn't just replace one group who were losers with another group who were losers, a mindset that is very hard to overcome.

With the help of Thomas Merton, Cynthia Bourgeault, Richard Rohr, Thich Nhat Hanh and so many others, I am working on it. I am still working on it.

I am seeing that we are all one, underneath it all. All kin.

And so now, I worry less about if anyone else has the wrong idea and worry more about whether or not I have the wrong idea. With Thomas Merton I say: let me be concerned more with the war like parts of myself than what I can see in others.

I officiated a funeral recently. It was said of the deceased, "She loved in such a way as to help others grow, develop, blossom. She believed in us."

That is the kind of belief I pray for.

And belonging.

If we could just teach everyone that we each belong, just as we are. In a world that is increasingly and bitterly divided, the simple, faith-based proclamation is a radical step, "You belong. You matter. You shine."

Belief and Belonging. We have work to do.

We all have work to do.

Prayer

Your own thoughts can hurt you
far more than your worst enemies.
But once they are mastered, they will help you
more than father or mother, said the Buddha.

God, Love Supreme, Love Supreme,
I will master my thoughts,
with your help and grace.

I will soak in radical acceptance,
radical hope, radical love,
for myself and for all others.
With your help and grace.

The sun will rise tomorrow.
And my spirit will never be defeated.
Amen.

Reflection Questions

What helps you find communion with God?

What is the ultimate sense of belonging that you have in this world?

In whom do you believe?

How do your thoughts hurt you? How can you transform them?

Thomas Merton's Epiphany

Where can I find your Lord?
Your place is grand and undisclosed.
And where can I find you not?
Your glory is everywhere upon the earth. Judah Halevi

When my daughter, Nina, was nine years old she liked for me to read her a story every night before bed. Sometimes she read them to me. We engaged different kinds of stories. But for a long time, she wanted a story from the book, *My Grandfather's Blessings*. Maybe because the stories tended to be short and sweet. Mostly though, I think it is because the writer tends to focus on her own childhood, in New York City, when she was eight, nine, and ten years old.

I remember one that I read to her about when the child in the story, Rachel, was eight years old and she was walking down a crowded street in New York City, where she lived. She was feeling very confident because she had just been in school that week and was sent to a new class. The teacher told everyone in the class that they were there because they were special. And she told them that it meant that they were smarter than almost all the rest of the people in all of the United States.

Rachel and her mother were visiting a friend and shopping. In the middle of the commercial district, there were many people around them.

Rachel decided to tell her mom how special she was. Rachel told her mom how good it felt that she was recognized for her gifts and smarts and talents.

It did not go as Rachel thought it might. Her mother stopped her in the middle of the sidewalk and bent down to her, close.

"Rachel. Listen. I want you to do something very important. Look around at all of these people. Every single one of them knows something more about something than you will. Love, or how electricity works, or how to overcome fear. You must respect that, in order to live a full, loving life."

"Is it because they are grown-ups and I am a child?" Rachel asked her mother.

"No, it is because each life is precious and full of wisdom and insight and everyone has something that they can teach you."

As the story goes, Rachel never really forgot that. When she became a doctor as an adult, she remembered that the person in front of her, beside her, or behind her had something to teach her too; they all had wisdom inside them.

It is a lesson that I hope my Nina can truly remember and hear.

The world is full of stories about epiphanies and revelations. This is my favorite.

In Louisville, at the corner of Fourth and Walnut, in the center of the shopping district, I was suddenly overwhelmed with the realization that I loved all these people, that they were mine and I theirs, that we could not be alien to one another even though we were total strangers. It was like waking from a dream of separateness, of spurious self-isolation in a special world. . . ..

This sense of liberation from an illusory difference was such a relief and such a joy to me that I almost laughed out loud. . . .. I have the immense joy of being a member of a race in which God became incarnate. As if the sorrows and stupidities of the human condition could overwhelm me, now that I realize what we all are. And if only everybody could realize this! But it cannot be explained. There is no way of telling people that they are all walking around shining like the sun.

Then it was as if I suddenly saw the secret beauty of their hearts, the depths of their hearts where neither sin nor desire nor self-knowledge can reach, the core of their reality, the person that each one is in God's eyes. If only they could all see themselves as they really are. If only we could see each other that way all the time. There would be no more war, no more hatred, no more cruelty, no more greed. . ... But this cannot be seen, only believed and understood by a peculiar gift. (Merton 1966)

Prayer

You are loved.

Go to the altar of your life
in the place known only to you and your God.

Go there, like it is a monastic cell,
the kind the desert fathers
insisted was all you need to learn
everything you need to learn.

Go there and just be quiet
for long enough to hear something.

Maybe at first, the something
you hear will be nonsense
or nothing much to write home about.

But soon, the message will come,
clear as a waterfall, clear as the morning sun:

You are loved.
You are worthy.
You are precious.
You are enough.

You are the beloved and the beautiful
and you are enough.

Go. Be quiet. And know.

Amen.

Reflection Questions

If you could stop all the people on the street and tell them one thing (Merton wanted to stop them and tell them that they were beautiful and that they shine as bright as the sun), what would you want to tell them?

Write about an epiphany you've had. A big one. A small one.

What do you do to try to see the divine in every person?

Baby Suggs and the Blessing

*May the God of hope fill you with all joy and peace in
believing, so that by the power of the Holy Spirit you
may abound in hope. Romans 15:13*

I want to tell you my all-time favorite story.

Baby Suggs is the matriarch of a community of slaves and
freed slaves who left Kentucky for Ohio. Slavery broke her down,
but she was holy. Not ordained, just holy. And in Toni Morrison's
amazing book, *Beloved* (1987), Baby Suggs points us to a deep and
abiding sense of a life in the spirit. For the entire sermon, search the
Internet for Baby Suggs's Sermon.

When warm weather came, it began. Baby Suggs, followed by
every Black man, woman, and child who could make it through the
forest, went to the clearing. She had her walking stick and she perched
up on a rock and spoke to her community.

Hope.

Baby Suggs called for the children to come forth. She directed
them to let their mothers hear their laughter. There is nothing bet-

110

ter and nothing more defiantly hopeful than children's laughter. The children laughed long and loud!

Remembrance.

She called for the men to come forward. She urged them to dance. Dance. And they danced an antelope dance that they brought over from their once-upon-a-time freedom land, Africa. And the dancing was powerful and life-giving.

Grief.

Finally, Baby Suggs called the women forth and told them to cry. Cry. Cry for the living and the dead. Just cry.

Soon enough, like all good embodied spirituality, it all came together. Everyone began to shift. Children dancing. Men laughing. Women dancing and laughing and crying. No one really remembered what she had asked them to do, it just all blended together beautifully. Laughing, dancing, crying, were all just happening, and it was magical!

She put down her walking stick, after a time. And they knew she was ready. A silence fell. Out of that silence, speech emerged that went a bit like this.

Baby Suggs commanded the community as she looked toward the heavens, then to the people, staring deep within those close enough to see. She told them to love their shoulders. Hands. Eyes. Private parts. She told them to love their feet, their long necks, their lovely faces. She said that out there, no one loved anything about them, and that they must love themselves. She told them to love their bodies, their livers, their backs, and not to give it a second thought. She said that most importantly, they must love their hearts.

The whole scene is a powerful encapsulation of the faith that can come from a sense of resilience and imagination. In a book full of remarkable scenes, this one endures. Ritual and resistance fuel the flame of resilience and imagination.

Prayer

Prayer at the New Moon
May you be for us a moon of joy and happiness.
Let the young become strong and the grown man maintain his strength;
let the pregnant woman be delivered and the woman who has given birth suckle her child.
Let the stranger come to the end of his journey and those who remain at home dwell safely in their houses.
Let the flocks that go to feed in the pastures return happily.
May you be a moon of harvest and of calves.
May you be a moon of restoration and of good health.
A prayer of the Mensa people of Ethiopia. (2001)

Reflection Questions

What rituals do you engage in that help you experience grief, remembrance, and hope?

In what communal opportunities for grief, remembrance, and hope do you engage?

How do you love your heart?

Who has been a Baby Suggs for you? Maybe someone who isn't a trained or ordained minister, but who speaks and exudes *holy*.

A Deep Dive

How to Pray

I will praise the Lord no matter what. Psalm 34:1

Okay. So, prayer.

Ira Glass on *This American Life* once talked about going into a Baltimore synagogue to say the Kaddish for his mother, on the anniversary of her death.

He said that it is an odd but comforting prayer, because basically in the face of death, all you do is say a bunch of prayers about how great and good God is. He said that even though he doesn't go to synagogue all that much anymore, the prayer was oddly comforting. He knew it by heart, all the Hebrew words, and he could say it and he knew it meant something deep down Inside. There was something about the knowing that it had been recited thousands and thousands of times that gave it more power.

Glorified and sanctified be God's great name throughout the world, the Kaddish says over and over.

Prayers like this, memorized as clearly as the rhymes from our youth, may evoke a deep, abiding peace. Sometimes that peace comes from the words themselves, other times, from the knowing that so many others have recited these same words for generations upon generations.

But that doesn't work for everyone. What do you do if you are one who doesn't get moved by these scripted prayers? How do you pray?

I don't trust easy formulas too much. I think they probably take away important nuances. But I want to give you a formula for prayer that could help you when you come up short.

Silence. Listening. Emptying. Praising.

This formula will help you to be truly open to God's prompting.

In *Thoughts in Solitude*, Thomas Merton reminds us that if we pray, we should remain confident that God will hear us and attend to us. If we pray while planning our own kind of answer to our prayer, we are showing little confidence in God! So, it might be a good idea to remember to enter into prayer in this way.

SLEP. Sadly, it doesn't roll off the tongue. If I added another *e* in the middle, we'd have *sleep*, but that wouldn't work either. So, we're stuck with SLEP.

Silence. Listening. Emptying. Praising.

Silence.

Silence is God's language. This is the very heart of the contemplative path. But it is not just important for contemplatives. All who pray should begin in silence. Thomas Merton reminds us that when we know the world in silence, there is nothing that can separate us from the world, from others, from God. Once we've taken on silence, and operate out of that place, we can no longer even be separated from ourselves.

Listening.

So many patients confide in me and tell me that they have no one really to listen to them. Loneliness and social dislocation are two of my obsessions as a hospital chaplain. I'm struck by how few of us take intentional time to deeply listen to ourselves, much less others. Many have televisions on or Facebook close by as constant distractions. Perhaps there is discomfort in the listening—perhaps these distractions keep the mind-noise at bay. Constantly, our minds are chattering away. We are invited in prayer to listen and listen with our spiritual hearts. When we listen in prayer, we become present to what is, just as it is. Without judgment. We receive a dose of *The Real*, before our minds can start labeling and judging. In that moment of listening, our prayers become sacred ground.

Emptying.

I am a practitioner of centering prayer. The very heart of centering prayer involves the idea of emptying. The technical term is *kenosis*, which means *self-emptying*. Cynthia Bourgeault, who is associated with the Center for Action and Contemplation, suggests that the self-emptying of Christ is the model (Look her up on the Internet too; she's pretty awesome!). We let go of all that we cling to, all our attachments, to make space for God to fill us and use us. When we empty ourselves, we let go of all of our biases, all judgments, all pre-conceived notions about what is "right" and we invite what is. It is in these times of pure presence can we truly receive God's intent.

Praising.

The fourth and final part of prayer is praise. If we know in our hearts that we are intended to exist on this earthly realm to receive God's intent, and to allow a vessel through which the Divine works, we must trust and praise. We must lay out the things/attributes we so admire in our Beloved. We must exalt the holy one's name.

The Psalmist gets it right. Here is how Psalm 34: 1-7 puts it.

I will praise the Lord no matter what happens.
I will constantly speak of God's glories and grace.
I will boast of all God's kindness to me.
Let all who are discouraged take heart.
Let us praise the Lord together and exalt the name.
For I cried to God and God answered me!

God freed me from all my fears.

Others too were radiant at what God did for them.

Theirs was no downcast look of rejection!

This poor man cried to the Lord—and the Lord heard him and saved him out of his troubles.

The Mountain (Nesotaieux)

Rouse yourself! Rouse yourself! Rise up! Isaiah 51

When my daughter Nina was thirteen, we took a family trip to Estes Park. Standing on the front porch of the YMCA of the Rockies, Nina looked up, seeing Long's Peak or Nesotajeaux (Arapahoe) in both the distance, and right in front of us. She proclaimed, "What even are we, compared to the mountains? What are humans anyway? Who are we?"

Such a profound question from a rising teen.

Martin Laird, one of my favorite contemplative writers, speaks of the need to simply observe our thoughts and distractions when we are in contemplative prayer. We don't fight them off. We don't try to not have them at all. We observe them and note them before they become a video that we get sucked into. We watch the "video" but we do it as a witness; unaffected by its contents. No more chatter. The chatter may remain, but we rise above it. It becomes background noise that we do not focus on. No more evaluating and comparing. We cultivate the perspective of just looking on, without judgment. No more: "Am I doing it right?" Just steady, calm, liberating gaze. We gaze from that place deep within us that is neither object nor subject, just the place where the I and the divine are one; the place where all edges and boundaries blur.

He compares this steady, calm gaze of our thoughts and distractions to the mountain. The mountain has no say in what kind of weather comes its way. The mountain just observes, calm and steady. It remains unaffected. The weather is our thoughts. The mountain is that deepest place within each one of us, vast and silent and sacred.

What are humans? We think we're the weather, but we're really the mountain. It's a simple concept, but it's not easy. The brain was designed to figure stuff out. If it doesn't have something to work on, it makes stuff up. We can't simply stop our thoughts (the weather); but we can fortify our minds (the mountain) so we, too, are unaffected.

I once helped an elderly couple in the ICU. This veteran, accompanied by his Korean sweetheart from the war, was in his last minutes of life. She didn't speak much. But she told me he'd like a prayer as he was dying. I summed up Psalm 23, his favorite. "I will not fear even though I walk through the valley, God is with me. What should I fear?" I prayed and blessed them both.

I wish I had read 121, which goes like this. "I look to the hills; I look to the mountain. Where does my help come from? From the God who is always with me and always in that mountain and every other mountain, in every valley, in every grove."

I didn't read that, but I wish I had. For, after he died, she cried out, "He is gone to the mountain. He has gone to the mountain." I sat there, listening. She looked at me and said, "That's what we say in our family when someone dies: he's gone to the mountain."

Do we become the mountain in our death? Is that the only time we can find true peace? Why not cultivate the mountain in our lifetimes, while we are in the flesh?

Nina asked me, "What even are humans?"

We are the ones, like everything else, who will one day go to the mountain.

For now, there is the simple call: "Rouse yourself. Rouse yourself. Rise up. How beautiful upon the mountains are the feet of the messenger who announces peace, who brings good news, writes the prophet Isaiah." Isaiah 51:17-23

Who are we, we humans? The ones that can rouse ourselves and rise up. We have not yet gone to that mountain that the Korean woman taught me about, the final resting place. So, in the meantime, we might as well give up being the weather and be more like the mountain that we already are. We might as well rouse ourselves and announce peace and bring good news, the good news that we are loved and so is everyone else, and that we belong and so does everyone else.

Look upon the hills. Look upon the mountain. Walk on it, announcing peace and love. All of that we can do as we rise up, as we rouse ourselves.

But more than that, be the mountain; be that calm, steady, liberating, healing, loving gaze that comes from a place of vast stillness and silence and where the I and the divine merge into one. Because that is really, finally, what we humans are.

Prayer

May the holy endeavors of the past come to us with lessons of courage and hope.

May the radiance of this day cause us to look forward.

We bless thee O God for the tides of love that come down to us through unnumbered centuries, groping through the darkness of ignorance, struggling over the bitterness and hates of life, revealing to us age after age the better way, teaching us generation through generation that the paths of love are the paths of power; that the ways of peace are the ways of holiness.

Make us righteous within, purge our hearts of hatred, clear our minds of ignorance that we may be one with thy holy ones of all ages, one with thee, one with all humanity, now and forever.

Amen. (Jones 1927)

Reflection Questions

How are you like the weather? How are you like the mountain?

How do you rouse yourself?

What is your view of the human animal? Or, what even are we humans?

One Inspiring COVID Scene

Though I walk through the valley of the shadow of death, I will fear nothing. Psalm 23

It was a Friday night about 7:00 pm. Shift change is a hectic time for nurses in a hospital. At shift change, the day nurse wants to give report and get out. The night nurse wants to know what happening and get started. But this COVID scene was seriously different, with all the PAPR and the N-95s and the sealed off doors.

You see, this was a COVID floor. This acronym had already become an everyday word for us. Corona Virus Disease 2019, (shortened to COVID-19 and often just COVID) permeated everyone's reality. Fear and anxiety around the virus, the misinformation, the fake news, all complicated everyone's feelings about this. For the first time in our lives, we were truly beginning to understand the term *pandemic*.

She was older, much older, and had just been in the hospital a few hours. The nurse told me that part of the family was desperately trying to find flight tickets from a sophisticated southern city and the other part was in a cosmopolitan beach town in Sunny California. "But," the nurse told me, "I don't think it will matter. If they get here at midnight or tomorrow morning, it will be too late."

With the southern family on the phone, the day charge nurse went into action, connecting the west coast family and transferring it to the room phone. A nurse helped me get my PAPR on and the night charge and I went into the room to make sure the call was coming through. I told the family I'd read a Psalm and say a prayer while they were getting themselves situated to spend time with her.

Such an emotional time. The logistics of getting to her bedside while she was still alive called for some creativity on all our parts, something we have learned a lot about during this pandemic. What I witnessed this night—what I was blessed to be a part of—reminded and reaffirmed my position, and how the Divine shows up for us.

The day charge nurse, Ellie, held the patient's hand and looked her in the eye, and for the next 45 minutes took her turn holding the phone up to the patient's ear, ensuring that she would not be alone.

"Is her hearing aid in?" one family member asked. Nervous and frustrated that they couldn't do more, we all assured them that it was.

The night charge nurse, Jill, stroked the patient's hair and when it was Jill's turn, she held the phone up to the patient's ear, lovingly holding the space necessary for the patient to connect with the family at her final moments. I held her other hand, on the other side of the bed from those two and held up the phone to her ear periodically too. Every once in a while, when there was a pause in any dialogue, I'd read Psalm 46 or 23, or say a silent prayer while the family spoke.

And then about 35 minutes into it all, the family mentioned that she had grown up on big band music. Oh yes! Oh yes! "Then there shall be music!" Quickly, a phone was procured, an app opened, and just like that, big band music filled the room!

The family knew they were heard and supported, and we felt lucky just to be instruments during this sacred time.

Jill cried sometimes. Ellie cried sometimes. They could have justifiably been doing other things on that floor, tending to other important matters. But they would not let that woman die alone and if that family wanted to be on that phone for 45 minutes, they were going to be there for that. They were going to show up, the best they could in that moment. Love in action in that moment was holding a phone so her nephew could pray with her, her grandchildren could say goodbye, and the rest of the family could connect in ways that left nothing unsaid.

When the patient took her final breath, she was surrounded by love. She was held, even from great distances, by her family and we, her surrogate family, gave her loving touch—the gift of held hands.

I stayed on the phone to discuss next steps, and the family was grateful. They asked me to thank both nurses for their love, support, and dedication.

Ellie went home.

Jill started her shift in earnest.

It was over.

Prayer

PSALM 23

The Lord is my shepherd; I shall not want.

He maketh me to lie down in green pastures: he leadeth me beside the still waters.

He restoreth my soul: he leadeth me in the paths of righteousness for his name's sake.

Yea, though I walk through the valley of the shadow of death, I will fear no evil: for thou art with me; thy rod and thy staff they comfort me.

Thou preparest a table before me in the presence of mine enemies: thou anointest my head with oil; my cup runneth over.

Surely goodness and mercy shall follow me all the days of my life: and I will dwell in the house of the Lord forever.

Reflection Questions

How does music soothe your soul?

What about other arts?

What would you like at your deathbed? Have you talked to your family and loved ones about your wishes? Write them down and share them.

What part of Psalm 23 most speaks to you? Why?

But Mostly Life is Like This

Do all the normal things in life. Come and go. Look. Listen. Smell. Touch. Taste. Pass your time in simple conversation but let the mind not stray from oneness.
Buddhist

While I was still in seminary, I thought about the sacred ordinary. How could I capture it? And this little reflection came to me after visiting Solomons Island, Maryland, right on the Chesapeake Bay. I wrote it a long time ago and Skinner House Books published it in a little meditation manual called, *How We Are Called* (2002). I think it captures a bit of how life looks when the ordinary becomes sacred.

Sometimes life is like this:

A minister friend, Meg, was invited to sit in front of a forum involving two groups that, truth be told, would rather the other not exist. One side spoke and shouted. The other side spoke and shouted. Words passed like light—invasive and all-encompassing but little understood. Exhausted, they turned to Meg. Have you anything to add?

Meg rose. "If you are in this camp, God loves you. If you are in that camp, God loves you." And then she sat down.

Grace abounds, grace abounds.

And sometimes life is like this:

I once went to a meeting with my District Executive in Delaware. Assuming I knew her position, I joked around with her. "Oh yes, I'm a UU Christian, but my Christology is appropriately low."

"What is wrong with a high Christology?" she asked.

Two weeks later, I learned that she left our place for a Catholic place. Assuming I knew her position, I forgot to let her own voice speak. Assuming I knew her position, I forgot to invite her into conversation.

Domination abounds. Domination abounds.

But mostly life is like this:

On a Thursday afternoon, books in hand, I said to the one I value and trust: Should we go to the water for a day? Spend some time on the Chesapeake Bay? Yes, I think so. We drove. She sang the songs of her childhood. We watched the sunset. We heard a dog bark. The boats slowly made their way under the bridge. A navy pilot navigated his craft, as he has always done. The woman at the Back Creek Inn gave us directions to a café, where we were served laughter and wine.

Life abounds. Life abounds.

Prayer

May you know that you are surrounded by love.

May you feel God's grace and peace, today, tonight, tomorrow.

May you know that you are not alone.

May you find the right path, the one just for you.

May you know that you are blessed and a blessing.

May your light shine, now and always.
Amen.

Reflection Questions

How does your faith speak to the need to find common ground even with those that you find difficult to agree with?

What is the great passion of your life, so that it abounds, so that you flourish?

What is your view of confession and reconciliation?

The Face

The fullness of joy is to behold God in everything.
Julian of Norwich

Emanuel Levinas was a Jewish philosopher who lived and taught in France. He survived the Holocaust but many of his family members did not. His work is really complex, but there is one part that is most intriguing: His view of the human face. For Levinas, the face is the source of the irreducible dignity and humanity of others.

Before we can make any label, the face signifies the place where "God passes" and thus orders us, with or without words, to refrain from killing. The face speaks the words: Thou Shall Not Kill. In this way, the face is very powerful. It refuses typologies. And what enables the face to have such power? God's presence in the face of the other.

The face is not just powerful. It also is extremely vulnerable. It is naked. It is completely exposed. It is hungry. It is thirsty. And in the face of that vulnerability, we become human by responding to the needs of the other. If they are hungry, we feed them. If they are thirsty, we give them a drink. The face of the other calls us into being and we respond, and in the responding we find out who we really are.

The face is a sacrament. It is a revelation of God. It is the word of God. And in the face of the other, all we can say is: *I behold you*, as Abraham said when God was speaking to him about the sacrifice of Isaac. *I am fully present*, as Moses said to the burning bush.

128

The face is that through which and in which the Invisible One becomes visible and enters into relationship with us. The dimension of the divine opens forth from the human face. Because of this, we must engage the other as truly unknowable, as mysterious as the very idea of God. And because of this Levinas is always going to say that when we confront the face of the other, we are always inferior. Why? Because we are in the presence of God.

Richard Rohr rightly says that for Levinas the face is the only thing powerful enough to covert us.

I think Rohr is right. And so I've asked myself: To what are we being converted? I say we are converted to the way of the non-violent Jesus: presence, peace, and compassion.

Presence.

Radical presence. Uninterrupted. Non-distracted presence, as we come to see that we are in the presence of the divine.

Peace.

Radical peace. As we confront the message of the face of the other, the divine face of the other, we can hear the message from the ages and from the depths: thou shall not kill.

Curiosity. Courage. Compassion.

As we find ourselves in the presence of the face of the other, we engage with open, non-judgmental curiosity about the needs of the person in front of us. We find the courage to be hospitable in the face of that need. And our heart of compassion grows.

Prayer

You are the forest. You are the great trees.
You are the birds and the beats playing within.
Oh, Lord, white as jasmine,
You who fill and are filled.
Why don't you show me your Face?
Akka Mahadevi, Vedanta

Reflection Questions

When you think of the vulnerable face, what comes to mind? What have you learned about the face as a result of its vulnerability? About humans? About yourself and your face? About your beloved(s)?

When you think of the powerful face, what comes to mind? What have you learned about the face as a result of its power? About humans? About yourself and your face? About your beloved(s)?

When you think of the pandemic and the masked face, what comes to mind? What have you learned about the face as a result of its masking? About humans? About yourself and your mask? About your beloved(s)?

When you think of the suffering face, what comes to mind? What have you learned about the face as a result of its suffering? About humans? About yourself and your face? About your beloved(s)?

If you would like, draw the face of God. Of the Goddess. Of the sacred mystery.

If your spiritual journey, if your life, if your illness had a face, what would the face look like? Describe it. Draw it.

Go Ahead Cast the First Stone

The Kingdom is within you, and whoever knows oneself will find it. Know that you are in God and God is in you. Jesus. The Gospel of Thomas. Saying 3.

The world's typical playbook has always and forever been about power. About getting what is yours. No matter what. No matter the cost. No matter who gets hurt.

The playbook pits us one against the other. A zero-sum game of winners and losers.

The playbook says: Look out for number one. Trust no one. Go it alone.

And into this competitive, dog-eat-dog, worldly playbook comes this half-mad, visionary, healer, going on and on about what the kingdom of God looks like. Going on and on about love and compassion and healing and peace. And forever and always hanging out with prostitutes and Canaanites and women and tax collectors. Whispering, shouting, the whole time: *This is what I'm talking about—the beloved community!* He's insisting over and over: *the kingdom of God is full of rejects and outcasts and losers.* Those are the ones on the margins. Those are the ones Jesus loved and hung out with. Because those on the margins, the rejects and losers, are the ones whose hearts are open.

They are the ones who are able to see the Beloved, the holy One, in the face of those right in front of them.

Would you like an example?

One day, while teaching in the temple, a group of guardians of the law came to Jesus and presented to him a woman caught in the act of adultery.

They said to Jesus, "The law says that we must stone her. What do you say?"

In response, Jesus knelt down and began to write and draw with his finger on the floor.

I like to imagine in that moment that he was writing: *Forgive them, Abba, they really don't have the slightest clue what they are doing.*

Whatever he was writing, Jesus finally responded, saying, "Let the one without sin cast the first stone. Go ahead."

Jesus went back to writing. This time I imagine him writing: *What am I supposed to do with these people?*

When he looked up all of the accusers were gone. But the woman accused of adultery was still there, untouched. Jesus said to her, "You're still here!"

She said, "Yes, Here I am!"

Jesus said, "Well, above all love. I am glad you are still here. I am glad you are still alive. Now, go, get yourself together, and be at peace. You are loved. God go with you."

The authorities were always having trouble seeing the Beloved in the face of the ones in front of them. Jesus was always reminding them to look deeper.

I want so often to pray: God, make us all humanists, by which I mean committed to the human right in front of us. The human who is a stranger. The human we'll never meet. A deep and abiding commitment to the humans and all of creation. Seeing the Beloved, seeing You in all your glory and all your pathos, in the outcasts, the rejects, the forgotten, the tortured, the lost, the confused, the mangled, the hated. And let us, in our moment of rejection and in our moment of greatest accomplishment, see You in our own outcastedness, our own rejectedness, our forgottenness, our tortured parts, our lost parts, our confused parts, our mangled parts, our hated parts. Give us courage to hold them up to the light, cupped in our hands, so that in that deep recognition, we see how much these give us compassion and empathy and love, for all of creation.

When Bonhoeffer was imprisoned, he wrote in a letter that only the suffering God can help. In the outcasts, the rejects, the forgotten, God is fully present, alive, calling to us.

Archbishop Oscar Romero, of El Salvador, was converted to the God of nonviolence upon seeing the grave of a martyred, assassinated priest. From then on, he saw Christ in the eyes of the poor and the homeless children, all around him. He saw them fresh and anew and saw them through the eyes of love. In the naked, the distraught, the imprisoned, the tortured, there was Christ and his second, third, fourth coming, over and over, calling us to a fellowship of love and brotherhood and sisterhood. Siblings, all.

You know the bumper sticker that says: *Jesus is coming! Look busy!* Romero and Bonhoeffer and so many others remind us that Jesus comes back all the time. Just not like everyone imagines. Rather, Jesus comes back in the face of the despised and the forgotten.

In the outcast, Romero and Bonhoeffer saw the Holy One. We are invited to do the same.

The beloved community, the kingdom of God. Right here in our midst, right now in our time.

God, for your sake, make us all humanists.

Mother Earth Father Sky,
Holy One Who Loves Fiercely,

We praise your name. It is hallowed.

You are here. You are there.

The mountain is your dwelling.
The cloud. The river. The deepest canyon.

You are here. You are there.

And you decided of all places,
to live in the soul of each bit of creation,
my soul. Yours. And yes even yours.

On earth as it is in heaven, let love reign.

Give each just enough,
enough rice, enough beans,
enough laughter, enough courage,
enough peace.

How often we miss the mark!
How often we fall flat!
You are there to catch us.

Give us the heart and compassion
to catch others as you catch us.

Oh, the distractions.

Oh, the trouble we can find.
Lead us to the path of peace,
despite ourselves!

Yours is every blade of grass,
every snowfall, every mountain slope,
every bumble bee, every drop of honey.
It's all yours. It's all love.
And we say thank you God, for all of it.

Amen.

Reflection Questions

What does the story of Jesus and the adulteress woman say to you?

When have you been an outcast? Who befriended you at that time?

How have you befriended the stranger, the outcast, the forgotten?

The Fugitive

I see my Beloved with the eyes of my heart. For those with eyes to see, the Beloved is everywhere. He escapes those mosques, temples and churches where they try to imprison Him. Darshan Singh, Vedanta, Hindu

Henri Nouwen, the Dutch priest, tells a story that has long lived with me.

A fugitive comes upon a small village. Wishing to escape and hide from those who are hunting him, he enters the village. The people respond with a sense of hospitality and offer to house and protect him.

Inevitably, soldiers show up, demanding to know where the young fugitive is. They made threats. In fact, they said that the village would burn and every man in the village would be killed. The only thing that could stop that is if the villagers gave the fugitive to the soldiers by morning.

The villagers, distraught, went to the religious leader. They asked, "We don't know what to do. We are afraid and confused. Help us. You decide. Do we shelter the fugitive, or save ourselves and give him to the soldiers?"

The religious leader went to her room, to think and to pray. She was deeply torn. She decided to turn to sacred scripture. As morning was coming, she read these words. "Better that one die than that the whole village is destroyed."

That settled it. She told the soldiers where the fugitive was hiding. The villagers were relieved. They celebrated with a feast. She wanted nothing to do with that. She went back to her room, overwhelmed with sadness.

That night an angel came to her and asked, "What have you done?"

She said, "I handed over the fugitive to the enemy."

Then the angel said, "But don't you know that you have handed over the Messiah?"

"How could I know?" the minister replied anxiously.

Then the angel said, "If, instead of reading your Bible, you had visited this young man just once and looked into his eyes, you would have known."

Stories like this land deeply within me. They remind me that no matter the bias, the judgment, the situation, I absolutely must look into the eyes of my siblings. And within their eyes, I may get a glimpse of the Divine, the Source, the Infinite, and I will know that we are One.

Prayer

How is Love Transforming Me?

How have I been transformed by love?

My wife, wealthier than I am, more sophisticated,
Smarter. Still loves me, despite it all.

And stayed with me when I didn't think anyone would or could.

And the kids, they groan at my dad jokes,
in just the right way.

And they keep coming back for more:
How do you fix a broken tomato?
Tomato Paste.

And once that happens enough times,
you begin to let the narrative go:
you're not good enough,
You're not measuring up,
what about our expectations,
how did you blow that start that you somehow got?

And you learn to replace it with:
Well, these four people like me,
love me even,
so there's that.

And don't even get me started on Gracie, the dog,
all grace, all the time.

And then, slowly, though you've been wrestling for so long:
call me Jacob, call me Thomas, let me touch the open spot,
before you commit, before you even venture a guess,
you begin to have this little stirring: there is in fact,
this love that will not let you go. That won't give up on you.

You could even call that love God, the holy one,
the divine, breath, spirit.

Even though for the longest time, the longest time,
you thought God was a puzzle to put together,
a formula to solve,
and that any love would only come,
could only come
from whatever you produce, whatever you publish,
whatever you accomplish.

And you could even say that once, a while back —
never mind the time of day,
the sun was going down, or the sun was coming up,
or it was high noon. I don't know.

(What is time, really?)

That the love that won't let me go whispered in your ear:
Accomplishments? What are you talking about?
I love you just as you are.
Goofy man. Silly man.

All the time I was here. Loving you.
Roger, you don't have to produce one thing.
What kind of colonial bullshit is that?

Just be. Just let the love soak in your bones.

Love your heart. That is the prize. As I love your heart.

Amen.

Reflection Questions

How is love transforming you?

What narratives in your mind might need a refresh?

How do you experience the love that will not let you go?

When and how have you learned something special and unique by looking into someone's face?

James Baldwin: Release, Release, Release

O LORD, hear my prayer, listen to my cry for mercy; in your faithfulness and righteousness come to my relief. Do not bring your servant into judgment, for no one living is righteous before you. The enemy pursues me, he crushes me to the ground; he makes me dwell in darkness like those long dead. Psalm 143: 1-3

The writer James Baldwin gave us so much insight on what it meant to be a Black man in mid-century America, what it meant to be a Black man and gay. His book *The Fire Next Time* is a world treasure. It is truly prophetic and it calls forth our better angels, for the good of all.

But it is his book *Notes of a Native Son* that I want to explore. One small scene that is a profound insight into the limitations one reaches in the midst of oppression and in the face of hatred, both individual and systemic.

Baldwin was in Trenton, New Jersey with a friend. He was told, "We don't serve negroes here." He snapped. He was spinning out of control and wanted to lash out. He says he wanted to crush the white faces that were crushing him. He walked a few blocks and found a fashionable restaurant where he knew that even an intervention by the blessed virgin would not get him served. He quickly walked in and sat down at a nearby table.

The waitress apologetically came over and said, "I'm sorry. We don't serve negroes here." The apologetic tone made it worse for Baldwin. He pretended like he couldn't hear her so she'd come closer. She did come closer but not by much. The phrase "we don't serve negroes here" was ringing in his head like a nightmare. He figured he would strike from a distance. The only thing on the table was a glass of water. He flung it at her. It missed and crashed into the mirror at the bar.

He came to and realized that he was in imminent danger. He ran for the door. His friend stood outside and told the white mob and later the cops that Baldwin went one way when Baldwin really went another way. His friend lied and saved Baldwin's life. Baldwin went home, heart pounding.

At home that night, Baldwin realized:

"I could not get over two facts, both equally difficult for the imagination to grasp, and one was that I could have been murdered. But the other was that I had been ready to commit murder. I saw nothing very clearly but I did see this: that my life, my real life, was in danger, and not from anything other people might do but from the hatred I carried in my own heart."

Protect your heart. In this season and always. Stay connected to your best self, your sacred source, and to all humanity.

Prayer

O Beyond Names,
We are often afraid, angry, enraged.
It is completely understandable.
It happens. So much is upside down,
And so much inequality and prejudice abounds.
And, dear God,
Do not let us carry that hatred,
that bitterness,
another moment.
Cleanse our hearts,
so we might be the world
we wish to see.
Amen.

Reflection Questions

Name your anger and rage and frustration. Say hi to it. Welcome it. And when you are ready let it go, tell it that it will not rule your days.

Injustice is hard. Hard to be a part of. Hard to watch. We so badly want to be the innocent ones in this particular dance. None of us are particularly innocent. Do you have regrets or shame that you also need to release?

How do you keep your energy grounded and centered in your highest aspirations and not in your deepest despair/frustrations?

One Day He Will Die

One day he will die but not anytime soon. He's sick but not knocking on heaven's door sick. Today, he wants to talk about retirement.

Retirement is an era, a time in life, that is often sought after, hoped for, and joked about. People plan for it. They save for it. They have lists upon lists of what they will do when they finally reach it.

Yet, once many get there, they find themselves without a title, without a mission, directionless and uncomfortable. Retirement brings a lot of discomfort and the need to face otherwise—or up until this point—unavoidable topics.

This is what he basically said to me:

"It is an adjustment. It is new. I'm not used to it yet.
I'm a psychotherapist and I follow the way.
The way of Jesus, the teachings of Jesus. The rabbi.

I studied with so and so in Chicago, my advisor.

145

Her whole thing was focus, and the life force behind prayer."

Then he started to cry, openly weeping, tears falling easy.

"I miss her. As soon as she spoke, I was won over. She knew.
She knew I got her and my work changed forever.
My dissertation changed the first time I heard her speak.
We stayed in touch all these years. Until the end. She died.
A grown man, I felt rudderless and lost, out to sea."

The tears flowed.
He simply could not believe, in that moment, that this woman, this icon, could leave him, throw him to the wolves to figure it out on his own.
And just like that he could not believe, in that moment, that his work, all that he had built, all he had loved, was abandoning him too.
Throwing him to the wolves to figure it out on his own.
Alone.

Prayer

God of infinite mercy

Remind us that we are given second chances,
third chances, fourth chances,
a thousand if we need them.

Every day is a new gift, from you O God.

So may we begin this day in gratitude
And thanksgiving and hope.

Be with all of us this day.

Give us peace and assurance
That you are with us always,
No matter what.

Amen.

Reflection Questions

Who were your great teachers?

What transitions are you facing that may be difficult to navigate?

When have you felt lost and out to sea? What happened?

What have you come to see about your great purpose in life?

What resonates about the patient and his experience with retirement?

A Deep Dive

The Four Chaplains

Allah is with those who are of service to others.
Quran 29:69

I love the story of the four chaplains.

It is a story near and dear to me, because it is about chaplains, but it is also dear to me because it is a profound moment of interfaith solidarity, interfaith cooperation.

It is a story about how to keep hope alive in the face of overwhelming odds. It is a story about love in the face of despair. And it is a story about faith and brotherhood—unity—and praying together even if you use different metaphors, even different language.

The Four Chaplains is an actual World War II account of the unity required when working side by side with those who are different from us.

The relatively new chaplains all held the rank of first lieutenant. They included Methodist minister, Rev. George L. Fox; Rabbi Alexander D. Goode of the Reform movement; Roman Catholic priest, Rev. John P. Washington; and Reformed Church in America minister, Rev. Clark V. Poling.

Their backgrounds, personalities, and faiths were different, although as a unifying trait, Goode, Poling, and Washington had all served as leaders in the Boy Scouts of America. They met at the Army's Chaplain School at Harvard, where they prepared for assignments in the European theater, sailing on board *USAT Dorchester* to report to their new assignments.

The Story.

It was the evening of February 2, 1943, and the *USAT Dorchester* was crowded to capacity, carrying 902 service men, merchant seamen, and civilian workers.

Once a luxury coastal liner, the 5,649-ton vessel had been converted into an Army transport ship. *Dorchester*, one of three ships in the SG-19 convoy, was moving steadily across the icy waters from Newfoundland toward an American base in Greenland. SG-19 was escorted by Coast Guard Cutters *Tampa*, *Escanaba*, and *Comanche*.

Hans J. Danielsen, the ship's captain, was concerned and cautious. Earlier the *Tampa* had detected a submarine with its sonar. Danielsen knew he was in dangerous waters even before he got the alarming information. German U-boats were constantly prowling these vital sea lanes, and several ships had already been blasted and sunk.

USAT Dorchester left St. John's Harbor on the way to Greenland in the fall of 1942 and was only 150 miles from its destination, but the captain ordered the men to sleep in their clothing and keep life jackets on. Many soldiers sleeping deep in the ship's hold disregarded the order because of the engine's heat. Others ignored it because the life jackets were uncomfortable.

A first brief aside.

I am fascinated by the fact that the *Dorchester*, this army transport ship, was originally a luxury coastal liner. The paradox!

It was built for laughter and lunches, for vacations and conversation. It was built to help facilitate relationships, enjoyment, and con-

150

nection. Now, it transported men, crowded and resolute, into a battle zone, a place of violence and disconnection.

I am struck by how much this mirrors the human experience. We were made from unity and made for brotherhood and sisterhood. But we have moved to a place of disconnection and competition and distrust.

Reverend Dr. Martin Luther King, Jr. reminds us that we are all caught up in a network of mutuality. Somehow, we've forgotten. We were born to be in relationship. We were born to explore that sense of mutuality. We have forgotten. Periodically, we remember. We began as one and our goal is oneness.

So that is the first aside. We were born to be in deep community, one with the other. We were not born to isolation, competition, destruction. We were born to love, to connect.

Back to the story.

During the early morning hours of February 3, 1943, at 12:55 a.m., the German submarine *U-223* off Newfoundland in the North Atlantic torpedoed the vessel, which knocked out the *Dorchester's* electrical system, leaving the ship dark. Panic set in among the men on board, many of them trapped below decks. The chaplains sought to calm the men and organize an orderly evacuation of the ship, and helped guide wounded men to safety.

One witness, Pvt. William B. Bednar, found himself floating in oil-smeared water surrounded by dead bodies and debris. "I could hear men crying, pleading, praying," Bednar recalls. "I could also hear the chaplains preaching courage. Their voices were the only thing that kept me going."

Another sailor, Petty Officer John J. Mahoney, tried to reenter his cabin but Rabbi Goode stopped him. Mahoney, concerned about the cold Arctic air, explained he had forgotten his gloves.

"Never mind," Goode responded. "I have two pairs." The rabbi then gave the petty officer his own gloves. In retrospect, Mahoney realized that Rabbi Goode was not conveniently carrying two pairs of gloves, and that the rabbi had decided not to leave the *Dorchester*.

As life jackets were passed out, the supply ran out before each man had one. The chaplains removed their own life jackets and gave them to others. They helped as many men as they could into lifeboats, and then linked arms and, saying prayers and singing hymns, went down with the ship.

The second aside. "Take my gloves," the Rabbi said.

What is life to us in the face of the reality that we too shall die?

"When the fear of death leaves us, the destructive craving for life leaves us too. We can then restrict our desires and our demands to our natural requirements. The dreams of power and happiness and luxury and far-off places, which are used to create artificial wants, no longer entice us. They have become ludicrous. So we shall use only what we really need, and shall no longer be prepared to go along with the lunacy of extravagance and waste. We do not even need solemn appeals for saving and moderation; for life itself is glorious, and here joy in existence can be had for nothing." (Moltmann 1983)

According to some reports, survivors could hear different languages mixed in the prayers of the chaplains, including Jewish prayers in Hebrew and Catholic prayers in Latin.

Some 230 of the 904 men aboard the ship were rescued. The rest of the men, including the four chaplains, died. On December 19, 1944, all four chaplains were posthumously awarded the Purple Heart and the Distinguished Service Cross.

This event was a catalyst for Americans to embrace interfaith understanding. Until the *Dorchester*, there was no mention in print of Catholics, Protestants, and Jews working together in this manner, especially in prayer. It was a transformational moment for America, the first time all three denominations were recognized by the mainstream population as serving together and with common purpose.

—

That is a good story, but most of us will never be called to such valor, to such sacrifice. What has this story to do with us?

First of all, we are made for unity, made for the brotherhood and sisterhood of all things. How are you living out that sense of connectedness? How are you doing with embracing community and love? And expressing it? And receiving it?

Secondly, each one of us will die. And each of us has this amazing miracle of being alive. So how do you want to live, given the fact of death. What do you want to be? Who do you want to be? Life is a flash. How do you keep hope alive in you? What does your faith look like, not your words, but the deep-down orientation of your faith that enables you to move through the days?

Third, these four chaplains prayed together, in Latin, in Hebrew, in English. In the face of a world that wishes to gain power by telling you that this group is evil and that group is not-even-human, in a world that wants to build walls, how are you staying in relationship with those who say the table is open, come and have lunch, come and sit a while? Tell me your story. Is not our purpose to find words that do not divide but unite, that do not create conflict but unity, that do not hurt but heal?

Finally, those chaplains encouraged the soldiers, kept them going. We rarely find ourselves in such a serious and dire situation. But we are constantly asked to chaplain one another. To accompany one another. To befriend and walk with one another in difficult times.

So, what can *that* look like? Henri Nouwen writes in one of his books about the importance of remembering those who really helped us. Often, that is not someone who gives advice or tries to fix things for us. More often than not, the one who really sticks with us is the one who can sit in the silence with us, who can share our pain and hold our hand without feeling any pressure to make it better. Every day, Nouwen says, we should look back on our day and ask: today, did I offer peace? Did I share words of encouragement? Did I love? These are the great questions that will help us build a life.

Annie Dillard's Typewriter

I became lost in the city of love, and there my soul was cleaned. Bulleh Shah

Spirituality, the religious way, is just to release that pulsating life-giving spirit of love inside that is aching to come out and dance and to waterski across the surface of a poem and wave at the author's name on the shore, and skip and dance and sing that love is all there is.

Annie Dillard was on an island somewhere in the northwest. She is the great essayist of the 20th century on nature and spirituality. As she was writing her book, she was in the zone. She was in that place where she was absorbed. Absorbed, by her task, her mission, her life's work, what we religious folks refer to as *her call* or *her vocation*.

What she had said *yes* to, what was hers to do and say, without which she would not even be alive.

What is that for you? What grabs you and will not let you go?

Annie Dillard was creating and in that process all kinds of things happen. And in this particular night, she had a dream, and in the dream, the typewriter caught on fire. Who could know what that is supposed to mean? Dreams have never actually been universally interpreted.

In her dream, she's absorbed. She's possessed. And somehow the typewriter is like an extension of her, like a blind man walking with his cane. Where does she end and the typewriter begin? There's no separation.

And she has no conception of success or failure. She has no sense of time. It is unbounded, yet somehow still embodied. She has no sense of praise or jeers.

The typewriter is ablaze. It is on fire. She pulls down the curtain to smother the flames, to no avail. She goes to fill a jar of water.

The flame continues, the fire goes on, but the typewriter is not consumed.

Everything Annie Dillard does, when she writes, when she observes, when she makes salad, she knows she is on holy ground. It's all holy. And she somehow has the gift of putting words to all of those odd thoughts and experiences. Not all of us can do that. We have other ways of being. But whatever we do, whatever our creativity, we are always on holy ground.

Does this story of something burning, but not consumed, bring forth any Bible story for you?

Moses and the burning bush.

The bush says: *Moses! Moses!*

And Moses says, "Here I am."

This "Here I am" is a special call out. I am fully present. I am ready.

Your life, whatever it is that is yours to do and say, your beingness calls out to you, calls you by name, and awaits your response: *Here I am.* And out of that *here I am* comes the creativity of your life, the creation of your path.

You are on holy ground.

And what does God, in the form of a burning bush, say to Moses?

Two things that are important: First, God promises, "I'll be with you. No matter where you go, no matter what happens, I'll be with you." That's number one.

And number two, when Moses asks, "Who exactly should I tell my people you are?"

God responds, "I am who I am. I am what I am."

I was sitting with Fr. Paul Wicker, 80 years old. He told me once he was doing some work up at Jewish hospital and he had a Catholic dying and this Rabbi had a congregant dying, a Jewish older person. After the deaths they sat together and talked. And the Rabbi said to Fr Paul, "You Catholics really require an image of heaven, an image of some place you are going after this thing called life."

"Yes," Fr Paul said, "we do have a lot of images, artistic and biblical, of what awaits. It is just how it has worked out."

The Rabbi said, "We don't so much have those things. It is not so important to us. We don't have any prescribed images about anything and most don't even care to speculate."

"I wonder why that is," Fr Paul said, respectfully.

And the Rabbi said, "You know when the burning bush talks to Moses and everyone says God responded *I am who I am. I am what I am.* In the Hebrew it is more like this: Go there and you'll see what I am. Go and you'll see who I am."

Jump in. Start. Walk. Go. And I'll be with you and you'll see what and who I am.

The typewriter eventually stops burning and it is not consumed, and Annie Dillard simply needs to dust away the ash and clean it up a bit and start typing again.

Prayer

May today there be peace within.
May you trust God that you are exactly where you
are meant to be.
May you not forget the infinite
possibilities that are born of faith.
May you use those gifts that you have received,
and pass on the love that has been given to you.
May you be content knowing you are a child of God.
Let this presence settle into your bones,
and allow your soul the freedom to sing,
dance, praise and love.
It is there for each and every one of us.
Amen.
(Attributed to Teresa of Avila)

Reflection Questions

What absorbs you?

What catches your typewriter on fire?

Write some *I am* affirmation statements about yourself.

First and Last

Then they came to Capernaum; and he asked them, "What were you arguing about on the way?" They were silent, for on the way they had argued with one another about who was the greatest. He sat down and said to them, "Whoever wants to be first must be last of all and servant of all." Then he took a little child and put it among them; and taking it in his arms, he said to them, "Whoever welcomes one such child in my name welcomes me, and whoever welcomes me welcomes not me but the one who sent me." The Gospel of Mark 9:33-37.

I could not believe what I was reading.

The most aggressive, hostile, dehumanizing rants imaginable. All over a speech, a speech by the President of the United States to be given to the nation's school children. Since the speech had been announced, certain conservatives had worked themselves into a tizzy over whether the speech would invite the children to become little socialists. Talk radio was on fire. Names were called. Incendiary language swirled.

At the time, Nicholas, my five-year-old son, attended a public Montessori school in Colorado Springs. There, the principal had decided on a compromise: at 2:30 p.m., on the speech day, the children would gather and watch the president's speech. If parents were somehow offended and wanted to excuse their children, they could do so.

Some liberal parents responded with rage. A listserv serving the school's PTA was buzzing with letters from liberal parents about Mr. Brilliant's compromise. The language to protest the principal's decision was cruel. It stripped the principal of his humanity.

For days, conservatives had lessened public discourse with scare tactics, had appealed to the very worst of our nature. And now, at my kids' school, some liberal parents were doing the same—attacking, crossing lines of decency, calling names. I could not believe what I was reading.

These were parents of children with whom my children were attending school and they were acting like schoolyard bullies. What in the world was going on?

Finally, on speech day, my son sat with his classmates and watched the president speak. For fifteen minutes the president told the children to do as well as they could. Nicholas sat transfixed. His eyes barely left the screen. When the president was done, along with his classmates, he clapped wildly and giggled with joy. I don't think it would have mattered at that moment if the president was liberal or conservative, Black or white, tall or short; his message—not his politics—had touched the children. Nicholas looked at his mother and said, "How did he know that we would all be sitting here?"

In that moment, all of the posturing, all of the bullying, all of the "arguing on the way" melted away in the simple, delighted, wonder-filled response of that five-year-old child, sitting in a downtown classroom in the shadow of Pike's Peak.

Nicholas seemed to be saying, "That guy treated me like I mattered, like I was important, talked to me about hope—I know he is important and he spoke just to me and my class. He noticed me. *Me.*" I could not believe what I was hearing—all of the cynical posturing gave way to a moment of pure goodness—an adult reaching out to children with care and compassion in his voice and a child's simple, awe-filled response.

Whoever wants to lead, needs to serve. Whoever wants to be great needs to be present with and hospitable to the most vulnerable among us—for example, the child.

In discussing Mark 9, Father John Dear says: What does Jesus say to us as we argue among ourselves. Let it all go. Let go of your ego, of your pride, your pursuit of honor and fame. Let go of your selfish demands upon others that they must serve you. Let go of control and domination of others. Let go of your problems, ambitions, career, greed, and need for achievement and accomplishment. Instead, serve one another. Serve the poor and the disenfranchised. Serve the hungry, the homeless, the sick, the imprisoned, the young, the elderly, the dying. Let go of your need to argue and follow me through humble, loving, unconditional service of suffering humanity. (Dear 2004)

I remember Rev. Meg Riley telling me about going to a meeting involving a group of gay Christians and a group of Christians who were working to "heal gay people of the disease of homosexuality." They had asked Meg to come and observe their meeting. Finally, after arguing about who was right—that is to say who is greatest— they became exhausted. They turned to Meg, "Have you anything to say?"

Meg, in the wisdom spoken of in all the great scriptures, said simply, "If you are gay, God loves you. If you are ex-gay, God loves you." And she sat down.

"Why are you arguing?" Meg seemed to ask. God's love embraces the whole human race—something worth celebrating, something that calls us into solidarity with our brothers and our sisters—into relationship, into awe and wonder and delight.

In many scenarios, when things get tough, we turn to arguments, control, domination. Jesus, in this passage, with the help of a little child, says to just let it go. And to turn to wonder, instead.

Let us then turn our hearts to prayer.

God, your love calls us to service. Remind us of the goodness that overcomes our cynicism, our power plays, our arguments, our rationality, our book-smarts, our ego, our desire to be great.

Remind us of the time we served and grew, when we moved beyond where we thought we were able to go.

Remind us of the times we have felt that we mattered to someone, some time we felt acknowledged and lifted up, because someone met us right where we were. Remind us of the solidarity that comes out of such experiences.

And when we forget, O God, set before us a child, so that we might welcome what we can know of amazement and wonder and goodness.

Amen.

How do you stay in touch with wonder and amazement?

What do you do when your ego gets in the way?

What do you think Jesus was saying about the way of the child as a guide for faith?

Francis and What Saves Us

There are no strangers here; Only friends you haven't yet met. William Butler Yeats

Here is what Francis of Assisi heard when the voice of God spoke to him. If you want to know my will, turn away from that which you previously oved. Once you do that, what once seemed sweet and desirable will become unbearable. The things that formerly made you shudder in disgust will bring you contentment.

Francis, alone in the countryside and trying to figure out his life, wondered what God was calling him to be and to do with his life. In almost the same moment, he met a leper. In those days, lepers rang a bell to announce their coming wherever they went, but this one had none. Coincidentally, Francis was deeply afraid of lepers, and yet, something stirred in him that said for him to greet this leper, rather than scurry away from him. In fact, he greeted him with the kiss of peace and embraced him.

Francis had always had an overwhelming horror of lepers. Here is how Francis described it in his testimony, "I began doing penance in this way: for when I was in sin, it seemed too bitter to me to see lepers. And the Lord himself led me among them and I showed mercy to them. And when I left them, what had seemed bitter to me was turned into sweetness of soul and body. And afterwards I delay a little and left the world" (1226).

And in the embracing, that he had in fact embraced none other than his Lord, Jesus.

First bit of lesson: Before we get to the modern-day lepers out there, maybe there is a part of you, hidden in shame, that you want to hide from the world. Francis calls us to confront our fears and go to that place, embrace that place, maybe it is the part of you that feels inadequate, feels out of control, or chaotic, or goofy or awkward, or whatever. Get off your horse, as Francis did, walk towards that part of you, embrace and see that it too is beloved of God. Greet it and embrace it; encourage those parts forth. Get comfortable with them.

Second bit of lesson: What does Francis do here? Before he considered the leper beneath him, sub-human, horrifying, scary, someone who was defined as their illness, their category, their label, he saw him as fully human. Upon meeting him, he sees them in their full humanity, and not just that, but as the beloved of God, as Christ himself.

Third bit of lesson: The leper, without question, is the absolute margins of society. They are without power, without privilege, without status, without proper documentation, without the right language. They are completely in the shadows. Francis was called to be with them, and the Franciscans, which he founded, obviously, soon became known as the ones who cared for the lepers. The call put him right in the midst of the margins, and he calls on the powerful to pursue peace, to put down their rifles and their guns and to embrace the ones without power on the margins. Hear me clear: Francis is Oscar Romero, using his voice to tell the soldiers to put down their guns. Francis is Daniel Berrgan and John Dear walking into the military site and attempting to dismantle the bombs. He is Thich Nhat Hanh telling the Americans to stop bombing Vietnam and to pursue peace.

He is not just trying to tell you to love the birds. He is here to tell you to pursue peace, and to sit with those who are homeless, to listen to them, to sit with the undocumented and to listen to them and to embrace them. He is here to say, we are invited to stand with the powerless, the marginalized, the disenfranchised. He's Cheney Goodman and Schwerner registering Black folks to vote in Mississippi who had been excluded from voting all those years and getting shot in the Summer of Freedom. He is every person who has ever stood up for those marginalized and without status.

Prayer

With beauty before me I walk
With beauty behind me I walk
With beauty above me I walk
With beauty around me I walk

With beauty before me I sing
With beauty behind me I sing
With beauty above me I sing
With beauty around me I sing

With love before me I pray
With love behind me I pray
With love above me I pray
With love around me I pray

Amen.

Reflection Questions

In what way does the gospel of your life, whatever that looks like, include being called to the margins to work for the powerless and the hated? It is your call. You have to decide where you are being called.

How can you see the next person and the next person as the Christ? But not just the ones you like, the ones that look and think and act like you, but all of them, how can you see them as the beloved of God?

Ring the Bell

For ye shall go out with joy, and be led forth with peace: the mountains and the hills shall break forth before you into singing, and all the trees of the field shall clap their hands. Isaiah 55:12

I went to see a colleague in the cancer center. We talked about a workshop we were leading together a little later in the year.

As I was leaving the cancer center, a group of four or five people were gathered close to the nurses' station.

A fellow had just finished his treatments and was "ringing the bell." He read the short little poem on the wall. He rang the bell and everyone (including me) clapped and clapped, cheering for his great accomplishment, and surviving this disease.

Sometimes the heart breaks, and hopefully breaks open to allow light in. Sometimes the heart swells, being glad for someone you never met and will likely never see again. Swells, the heart does, with pride and good wishes.

This is the work: to bear witness, and to cheer on the one you will never know, and to cheer on the ones you know especially well.

To keep cheering, to keep cheering, to keep cheering.

Then the broken heart heals just a bit. And the broken open heart connects with the goodness at the heart of all that is.

So many stops along the way.
So many detours.
So much not knowing,
and thinking I knew, but not.
Or thinking I did, but didn't.

And I still don't know fully, O God,
if I am on the right path.
But here you are and here I am.

Here I am! Heinini! I behold You.

And this night and this fireplace are enough.
The stars in their sky, enough.
The dog next to me, enough.

The menorah and the books
and the communion set and the candles,
all enough.

This is enough
and I thank you.
Amen.

Reflection Questions

How do you see yourself as a healing presence?

What is your sense of the work that is yours to do?

How are you cheering on others?

Loving Kindness

*I cling to you. Your goodness and your loving kindness
are my rock and my salvation. Psalm 68*

I remember a woman I spoke to in the hospital. She was saying all the right things. Her self-esteem seemed fine. Her resolve seemed fine. But she spoke of a melancholy within her spirit. She spoke of doubt and uncertainty.

And as we talked, it was clear that she was trying to say all the right things, be the right thing, do the right thing. She was working very hard.

But in the back of her soundtrack, the soundtrack of her life, were the words of her parents:

You weren't good enough.
You aren't good enough.
You won't be good enough.
Nothing you can do will be enough.

You are not right.
You are not put together properly.
You won't succeed.

Think about how exhausting that is. Think about how devastating that is. She was doing all she could to rewrite the narrative, but the narrative was stuck on a loop that was all about her inability to just be, to just be good enough.

She was religious. She went to church. She was a disciple. She was a good person.

But that narrative, it was always with her.

She was disoriented, in a big way. The map was all askew. The compass was not functioning. The GPS was off-kilter.

So much of those judgments—about ourselves and others—are based in anxiety and fear.

So much of the healing that must occur in our lives is a giving up of fear, of judgment, of comparison. And moving towards grace, and peace, and wholeness.

And we who are in the church must be a part of that liberating message, that love is at the heart of our entire enterprise and grace and mercy.

That God desires for us a sense of wholeness and well-being, shalom and peace, and loving kindness, towards ourselves and one another.

Look if I am a hospital chaplain and I start judging the addict because he's an addict, am I an ambassador of the God of peace? Am I a representative of the God of love and grace and mercy?

If I judge the addict, and if I judge the heart attack person because their diet was awful, or the person dealing with anorexia, am I an instrument of peace and love?

No, I remember in those moments my own struggles with bad choices. I call up within me a spirit of humility and connection and compassion.

I remember that so much of life is a combination of bad luck and bad timing.

So, I offer words of reassurance. I remind the person that they are stronger than they realize. I ask them to think about times when they overcame something that they thought would be impossible to overcome. I remind them of their own resources.

And, if they say "I don't have many resources right now. I don't have much hope or strength." I might gently remind them that that re-orientation is possible. Maybe not restoration. If a spouse has died, that spouse is not coming back. But reorientation is possible. They might very well remember a time when they somehow got through.

"Tell me about a terrible time, I might say." And once they're done, I'd ask, "How'd you recover?"

I cling to you. Your goodness and your loving kindness are my rock and my salvation.

Muhammad's Night Journey

"Exalted is the One who took the Servant by night from al-Masjid al-Haram to al-Masjid al- Aqsa, whose surroundings We have blessed, to show him of Our signs. Indeed, He is the Hearing, the Seeing." (Quran, 17:1)

I really like this story about Muhammad.

Muhammad is at his lowest point. His business is suffering. His beloved wife, his main source of consolation in this world, has died. And his uncle, who raised him, has also died.

One night in his sleep, having left his town, he prays: O, Most Merciful and Compassionate! You are the Lord of the oppressed and You are my Lord. I do not care for anything except Your pleasure. I seek refuge in Your light which illuminates all darkness. I pray that I should never incur Your wrath and displeasure. There is no strength or power except through You.

Jibril (Gabriel, the angel) visits Muhammad. Wakes him up. Takes him to a winged creature (Al-Buraq). Al-Buraq takes Muhammad to the Al-Aqsa mosque in Jerusalem. At some point, Jibril takes Muhammad's heart out of his chest and washes it with water. And then, there is this remarkable image. Jibril brings forth a vessel of gold, filled with wisdom and faith, and pours it into Muhammad's heart.

Al-Buraq has gone as far as he can, but Jibril keeps Muhammad company as they travel to the seven heavens. There, they meet Jesus, Moses, Abraham, John the Baptist and others. At each heaven, there is a gate and a watcher.

The watcher says at each heaven, "Who goes there?"

"It is I Jibril," responds the angel.

The watcher always asks, "Who is with you?"

"Muhammad," the angel replies.

In response, the watcher asks a most important question, "Has he been called?"

"Yes. Yes, he has." Jibril responds.

The watcher relents, "Wonderful! Then proceed."

At every heaven, the Prophet encounters a prophet. In the first heaven, he meets Adam, the father of mankind. The Prophet greets Adam with the greetings of peace. Delighted to see the greatest of his descendants, Adam replies, "Welcome my son, welcome O Prophet of Allah!"

At each heaven he sees different pillars of the faiths: Jesus and John, Aaron, Enoch and so on. They all celebrate seeing their brother in faith. In the sixth heaven, Muhammad encounters Moses and in the seventh, the great Abraham who is honored as one who sincerely yearns for and seeks the unity of God.

It is a cloud of witnesses, a brotherhood and sisterhood of goodness and mutuality. (I imagine Sarah laughing with joy and wonder and Hagar tearing up with pride and love.)

Muhammad ascends to heaven on his own, having been cheered on and encouraged, and accompanied along the way. The last part is his alone. He is in the presence of Allah. They converse. They talk.

Muhammad asks Allah, "How often must my people pray?"

"Fifty times a day," responds Allah, unmoved.

Muhammad says, "So it shall be."

On the way down, Muhammad comes upon Moses.

Moses asks Muhammad, "What did you talk about?"

"I asked how often my people should pray," Muhammad answers without much thought.

Moses is curious. "Oh, what did God say?"

Muhammad tells him, "Fifty times a day," somewhat nonchalantly.

Moses is not convinced, "Not possible. Go back and talk some more."

The next number was 40. Then 30. And it went on like this until Muhammad told Moses that God said five times a day. And Muhammad said, "I'm not going back. Five it is."

What a powerful, wondrous story! The gold in the vessel of faith and wisdom. The cloud of witnesses cheering Muhammad on. And Moses and Muhammad and Allah/God all collaborating to come to a decent number of times per day to pray. It is one of my favorite stories in all of religious literature.

Final Thought

I love that at his lowest, when all might be lost, when he was in the midst of grief and disorientation, Muhammad is taken on this journey. It is a story of hope, at the end of the day.

Only and everything matters
The divine, in her essence
And all the little pieces too.
The little piece that is me.
The little piece that is you.
The bird and the tree.
The bird holding the fish,
Both and.
The owl and the mouse.
The church, the son and the moon.
The river and the sea.
The seeker and the finder.
The lost and the not so lost.
Your anger and your tears.
Your first smile and your last.
All of it, divine.
All of it belongs.
Amen.

Reflection Questions

If you had a vessel full of gold with your wisdom and faith in it, how would you describe the contents?

What is in your container of gold? Let's say you could gift someone a container that held your faith and your wisdom. What would be inside your container?

Who is walking with you? Who is cheering you on? Who is among your cloud of witnesses?

Have you ever tried praying a consistent number of times every day? How was that for you? Would you consider taking that on?

Fighting for So Long

Learn to do what is good. Seek justice. Correct the
oppressor. Defend the rights of the fatherless. Plead
the widow's cause. Isaiah 1:17

Because I've been fighting for so long and insisting
and persisting
and persnickety
and resisting
and fighting for so long

I forgot to notice along the way that I too am loved
that I too am graced
that I too am hurt
and scattered and broken and confused
and that I too am loved.

It's easier after all to think about the injustices out there and
ignore the tears in here
    it's easier to find a distraction to climb a hill that is not mine and
ignore the tears in here.
    and I don't know where any of it leads but I think I'll spread a
little light, share a little light
    ask a little light to come around,

call it God, call it love, call it thou, call it peace,
call it unnamable, call it what you will
I'm over here asking it to light me up
I am loved, I am loved, I am loved.

Sweet holy spirit,
We pause before another day of exploration.

First, to give thanks that we are alive and breathing
and to give thanks for the moon and the sun
and the bright blue sky.

We pause to open our hearts
to open our minds
to be receptive to the wisdom this day will bring us.

We pause to remember the sacred center
of our bodies and our spirits.

To remember the goodness at the heart of all creation,
including ourselves.
That purposeful goodness from which we come,
in which we live our fullest,
to which we shall at last return.

There is no other day.
no other hour
no other people
no other life
everything we need is here
all the pieces
all the possibilities
the ideas and the partners
no saints or heroes required
no perfect plans

no perfect people
only
the willingness to speak and to hear
to laugh
to explore
the willing heart
of each one we encounter today
the heart filled with wonder
we each of us are stumbling
and bumbling
we each are forgiven
and we each forgive
thank you, God, thank you spirit

we show up
we've shown up

these are the ingredients
we need today
for healing
for change
for life
they are all here
and here is enough
for praise and thanksgiving
and the work set before us.
Let us begin the day in joy and peace.

Amen.

Reflection Questions

As you think about your spiritual journey, when have you felt you were most resistant? What happened? And what was that about?

How did you come to a place where you felt loved?

How did you come to a place of self-acceptance and self-appreciation?

Hold Ever So Gently the Beauty and Dignity of the Broken Heart in Front of You

I have blessed you so that you might be a blessing to each and everyone. Genesis 12:2

Be willing to show up. I know. I know. Everyone says it. It is a cliché. Show up for your kid, even if you don't feel like it. And your mom too. Your old man, your cousin. Of course, your beloved and your neighbor. Mostly, yourself. Show up for yourself.

If you are to show up, you have to know the you that is showing up, the *you* who you are. This is the second thing. The you who is showing up, of course, you and only you know. But one thing I know for sure is that the you that is showing up is loved beyond measure.

You are loved. Any good worthwhile theology insists upon it. You are loved. You are precious and worthwhile. You belong. Act from there. Then you can show up with grace and love and peace.

Remember, to show up is to be spacious, so the other person can just be. To show up is to let the other person just breathe and talk and think and cry. And to be and bring forth this kind of spaciousness, you simply must develop a love affair with silence. In the silence you'll learn that you are loved. God's love. The wild earth's embrace. The Goddess's kiss. Pick an image, the eternal mystery loves you so that you might love in turn.

Call it what you will. Out of that love, you'll embrace the mystery of silence, and out of that embrace, you'll love yourself and the other and you'll see this is not really yours to fix or manage or take on, and you can hold ever so gently the beauty and dignity of the broken heart in front of you.

Now, this is key. Don't fix. Don't fix. Don't fix. Just sit. Just sit. Just sit. Sit longer than you think is needed and stay silent longer than you might like.

Get comfortable with awkward silence. Over time awkward silence grows into meaningful silence. To get there you take a right or a left at self-awareness until you hit the intersection of self-knowledge and humility. The gate at that intersection holds everything you need to know.

Saint Teresa of Avila, doctor of the church, was right, the Gate consists of self-awareness and humility. I hear you; your GPS is showing you the alleyway up ahead labeled *curiosity*. We are not there yet. One step at a time. Curiosity, courage, compassion, they'll come. They'll come. I promise. But for now, baby steps. Patience. First things first.

Love has the first and the last word. Sometimes, a spouse, a child, a partner, a best friend, their beloved one about to be left behind for a last time, will look at me and their eyes will speak: *I know I have to leave this hospital room eventually, but how do I do that? How do I go home alone, without them?*

Look, some questions do not have an answer. You just go ahead and do the next thing at whatever time you can do it. Love will not stand in the way of your deep grief. Love will let you stay bedside as long as you need.

Hold ever so gently the heartbreak right in front of you, yours and theirs, and the next thing, whatever that is, will be done.

Prayer

Pray for the one who is angry at God.
His wife is upstairs in critical care, basically alone,
being loved by nurses and docs and chaplains,
best we can. She will die. And he knows it.
If praying is your thing, go ahead and pray.
There is another one today, whose loved one is dying as well.
He, too, is mad. He's mad at the doctors for not trying
the latest recommendation from this president,
which is no kind of cure, no kind of treatment.
Sometimes, grief looks like lashing out at anything and anyone.
Keep him in your heart, if that is your thing. Hold him in the Light.
Thank a nurse, if you'd like to do something a bit more concrete.

People ask me: Where have you seen the holy in this COVID-madness?
Once, approaching midnight, a nurse lovingly helped a wife
put on her PAPR, knowing this would be the last time she saw him
alive.
Later, the nurse took it off. The grieving, lost wife looked at me
and said: Chaplain, what more should I have done? What now?
What now? It is the only question, the most important thing.
Bring solace where you can in the way you can.
Bring a word of consolation, sing a song of hope.
Sit in silence, and hold in your heart's hands the angry one,
the grieving one, the lost one, the sick one, the left behind.
A long while ago, my loving uncle visited my family in Colorado.
He was from Winston-Salem. My 7-year-old, shy,
hid behind a chair. His smile brought her out.
As he was leaving, he said: Norah, God has great things in store for
you.
She never forgot it. What now? Bless a child, and then another.

There is pain in this world. And there is loss. There are tears upon tears.

So too is there hope. So too is there a blessing, never forgotten.

Keep choosing to bless the world. From the start, the world needed love.

Your love. Your peace. Your blessing. And forever, the world will need you, just as you are, just as you are becoming, to bless it and keep it in your heart.

Amen.

Reflection Questions

Imagine those who love you seated in a circle around you as you sit in a chair in the middle. Each person has been asked to say a few words about what they love about you. What would they say?

Now picture each one, in turn, sitting in the middle as the rest of you are circled around. What would you say about each one of your beloveds?

Try to find occasions to tell them. And yourself too!

The Parables Explained? Never!

He spoke in parables like this, all the time, in all the places. But later, at night, with only the disciples around, he explained everything. Mark 4:34

Would I have wanted to attend the post-party, where everything is explained? Imagine the dialogue.

Jesus: Look, it's a bit of a joke. Everyone knows that mustard seeds are the biggest nuisance. When the mustard seed grows into a plant, it gets all entangled in the orderly planting systems of the elite and disrupts the status quo. It's a trickster parable, get it?

Random Disciple 1: Oh, we were just talking about this amongst ourselves. We all agreed that it was because mustard seeds are super tiny, like us, but grow into something useful and helpful and tasty.

Jesus: Of course, that is part of it. But it's really about disruption of the normative paradigm and actuating new realities in a mind-numbingly, soul crushing world.

Random Disciple 2: I can see it. Yes, that makes a lot of sense.

Would I have wanted to be sitting around that room?

I like my parables with a healthy dose of koan-like mystery. I don't want them explained. I want them to work on me.

When I was 21, or 22 and finishing up college while putting away the religion of my formative years, I wanted the parables to "mean" something, to have a clear moral compass.

Today, I want the parables to read me as much as I read them. To grab my heart and twist it around, and open it up. I no longer need them explained.

Now I want to trust myself as I walk into the house of mystery—unsure, uncertain, unconvinced, heart wide open, mouth sealed shut—the same way I walk into the room, as I did earlier tonight, of the fellow in his late 60s, completely coherent, whose first words out his mouth were, "It's true. Tomorrow, I'm going to hospice. I'll never leave this building, well other than with a sheet over my head."

"Really? I had no idea. Tell me everything."

And all the stories come pouring out, and they are so much more than any explanation could possibly hold.

Prayer

O Great Mystery,
The Known Beyond All Knowing,

O that I might live without certainty,
that I might live in the questions of it all,
to be comfortable there,
to stay there and abide in it, the messiness of it,
The non-assurance of it

as you abide in me
though I know nothing of myself

as you abide in me
and your love and your grace
Even though I am lost and unsure and guarded
and all of it, messy, messy.

Thank you. And again, I say Thank you.
Amen.

Reflection Questions

What is your relationship with uncertainty?

What is your relationship with the need to know?

What is your relationship with trust?

What is the mysterious story at the heart of your being?

God Is with Us.

God Is with Us.

*"Can you fathom the mysteries of God?" The Book of
Job 11:7*

All I knew was that the page I got was some kind of cyclist versus an automobile trauma. Nothing more.

Monday, I worked my regular shift at the hospital. This go-round I was on the shift from 1-9:30 p.m. That night, I happened to be covering the pager for both hospitals, the one in the center of town and the one in the north part of town, where I had worked all day.

At 9:30, I got in my car and headed home. I live in the south part of town, so it was a long trip. About halfway home, fifteen minutes into my drive, I got a page from the hospital in the center of town. I drove towards that historic hospital building that I love.

I got there and learned that the cyclist, "Jack," in his late 40s, was on a bicycle. He had been hit by a car in a town three hours from our hospital. The family was expected in an hour to an hour and a half.

I waited. I got the phone number for the brother. After an hour or so, the brain surgeon had a very difficult conversation with the brother as he drove towards Colorado Springs, through mountain towns. "There is not much we can do. If on the remote chance your brother survived, he'd always be a vegetable." The brother was sure that the patient would not want to live like that, that he'd prefer to go to heaven and be reunited with their father who had died eight months earlier.

"Drive safely. Do not rush. We will all be here waiting for you. You all are in our prayers," I said as I hung up with the brother, after the doctor's conversation.

When the brother, Henry, arrived with his wife, the patient was transferred from the Emergency Department to the Critical Care Unit, a place where they could more comfortably say their goodbyes, as Jack began the journey towards death.

It took a while for the doctor to come in and oversee the removal of the ventilator. Jack was young and his heart was strong. He fought, just as he'd fought and played in life: vibrantly. As Jack's breathing slowed, Henry and his wife, Vivian, told stories about Jack, about how he loved to help out around the ranch, how he loved to call people on the phone asking for this or that. While Jack had a developmental disability, it never interfered with his connection with people. He worked every day, hard. And when he was a child, his knees were positioned in such a way that he was told he'd never walk, and yet he walked and ran throughout his life.

"I hate that this had to happen to Jack, so innocent, so pure," Vivian said at some point. "We love you, Jack. Always will."

Henry whispered, "You did so great. You were so great. It is time to rest."

After a time, Jack died. The doctor left. Henry and Vivian said their goodbyes and after twenty minutes, we all wrapped things up, talked funeral homes and next steps and I gave them a book on bereavement with my name and phone number in it and lots of articles about things like holidays and loss.

I went to my office, charted quickly. I was exhausted. I had started at 1 p.m. at our hospital up north and was finishing my day at our downtown hospital at 4 a.m. I shut off the lights in the office and walked to my car, three pagers attached to my belt.

To leave this hospital towards my home, I drive through old mansions in a part of town called The Old North End. A neighborhood could not contain more beauty. As I approached a major street, Uintah, my pager went off. *Oh boy*, I thought. On the pager was a simple phone number. The only problem was that my phone was dead. No charger. No juice. I had to make a decision. *Do I turn around and head the 8-10 blocks back to the hospital?* I turned on to Uintah. In front of me was a 7-11. *How busy can a 7-11 be at 4 a.m.* I thought to myself. *I'll ask the clerk there if I can borrow a phone to use. If he says no, I'll go back to Penrose.*

There were more cars than I would have ever guessed (Who knew?). I got out of my car, and coming out of the front door, right at that moment as I approached it, were none other than Vivian and Henry. "Oh my gosh," I said. "Hey, do you have a phone on you?"

"Yes, of course. Use Henry's." I called the hospital number. It was the charge nurse from CCU, where we had just spent the last few hours of Jack's life, bearing witness to the goodness at the heart of his being.

"Hey Roger. It's Nurse May. I just have a quick question about the details of the contact information for Henry, Jack's brother."

"Well, that should be easy. Here he is. Ask him directly." In the parking lot of the 7-11, I handed him the phone, gave him another final hug, hugged Vivian and was on my way.

Vivian said, as we departed, "God is with us. God is with us."

 Prayer

I will make a joyful noise.
The tambourine, for sure.
The trumpet, why not!
My singing voice. Yes!

I will sing your praises.
I will tell the story of your compassion.
I will run in the streets
and yell from the rooftops.

Such a world we live in.
Such beauty all around.
Such grace and love!

I will sing a new song.
Love will see us through.
I will sing a new song.
Laughter will save us.
I will sing a new song.
Everyone be free.

Amen.

Reflection Questions

Have you experienced a coincidence that sticks with you? Something that almost felt like a miracle? What is that story?

What is your sense of how God works in the world?

What are your names for the divine?

Which of those names are your favorite and why?

Christ's Table

But the fruit of the Spirit is love, joy, peace, forbearance, kindness, goodness, faithfulness, gentleness and self-control. Against such things there is no law. Galatians 5:22-23

The Monday and Tuesday before the inaugural in 2017, I was in Washington, DC. I was there with a group called Abolitionist Action Committee, a loose network of activists who seek to end the death penalty. We gathered, about 100 of us in all, to mark the 40th anniversary of the execution of Gary Gilmore in Utah, the reinstatement of the death penalty in the modern era.

I traveled to DC this time with my friend, Mike Martin, the Mennonite founder of RawTools, a faith-based nonprofit that converts guns into garden tools. *(Isaiah 2:4 They will hammer their swords into plowshares and their spears into pruning hooks. Nation will no longer fight against nation, nor train for war anymore.)*

Monday night, we gathered at Church of the Reformation, in the shadow of the US Supreme Court. People were there from all over to hear from those directly impacted by the death penalty—the 119th exoneree, Derek, who spent 20 years on death row wrongfully, a mother whose son was on death row in Virginia before being released to basically a life sentence, a woman whose father was murdered in front of her, and many others with their own varying stories. A spoken word poet from Philadelphia spoke of the death penalty, the cross, and the lynching tree. Shane Claiborne, a leading activist for nonviolence and for service to the poor, emceed the event.

He's my vote for the most interesting Christian around and author of *Executing Grace: How the Death Penalty Killed Jesus and Why It's Killing Us* (2016).

While they were speaking, outside on the small yard in front of the church, Mike, his father, and two blacksmiths took a rifle much like the one used by the state of Utah and turned it into a little garden tool. Mike and Fred founded RawTools, that I wrote about earlier.

I thought then about transformation. *God, turn my cynical heart into an instrument of your hope. Turn my weary heart into an instrument of your rest. Transform my anger. Turn around my ambition. Turn my violent heart into an instrument of your peace. Let me hammer away at my self-righteousness and turn it into something life-giving, like a garden tool.*

The next day, Tuesday morning, we gathered at the United Methodist building. I prayed aloud for all of us, and our country. We then all marched into the cold, rainy day where 18 brave souls, including Shane Claiborne and Derek, would be arrested for unfurling a sign on the Supreme Court steps that read: Stop Executions. The rest of us were on the sidewalk, praying, singing, chanting. And then we disbursed.

I will say that the most memorable part of the trip for me happened Monday morning. Mike Martin and his dad, Fred, and I were walking on the mall, being tourists. We went to the top of the Lincoln Memorial steps. Fred, a lifelong Mennonite surveyed all of the marble and granite of the buildings along the mall. "How different this empire looks from Christ's table, full of the poor and humble. How very different."

May Christ's table transform our hearts and our world.

Prayer

God, turn my cynical heart into an instrument of your hope.
Turn my weary heart into an instrument of your rest.
Transform my anger.
Turn around my ambition.
Turn my violent heart into an instrument of your peace.
Let me hammer away at my self-righteousness and turn it into something life giving, like a garden tool.

God, you have no hands. Use mine. Make me an instrument of peace.
God, you have no feet. Use mine. Let me walk with the stranger, the outsider, the forgotten.
God, you have no eyes. Use mine. So we both can see you reflected in every bit of creation.
Amen.

Reflection Questions

Can you draw Christ's table? Write about it. Write a poem. Craft a song.

What part of you is in need of transformation?

Where does your hope lie in making a change?

All Will Be Well

"Whosoever destroys one soul, it is as though he had destroyed the entire world. And whosoever saves a life, it is as though he had saved the entire world."
Hillel the Elder, Jerusalem Talmud Sanhedrin 4:1

I was a minister in Davenport for seven years or so, and I happened to be serving the church during the tenth anniversary of Matthew Shepherd's death. He was tortured and killed because he was gay and his death galvanized support for human rights and the dignity of all. Our church had a longstanding relationship with the Gay Men's Chorus, and so we decided to do a joint service between our church and the Metropolitan Community Church, a church that serves the gay, lesbian, bisexual, transgender community predominantly, on the Sunday closest to that anniversary. All was set. My music director was going to do a series of vignettes and readings from a play about Matthew Shepard's life and death. He had all that covered. And the pastor from the MCC Church was going to do a part. And I was going to do a part. And the Gay Men's Chorus was going to sing one song in between the readings. It was all set and basically my music person was in charge. I didn't even know which pieces he'd be doing from the play.

The Wednesday before, I got a call. The director of the Gay Men's Chorus told me that they wouldn't be able to sing after all. So many were going to be out of town, they felt they couldn't pull it off.

I went into a bit of a panic. This huge service was at risk. We'd look unprepared, amateurish, and this service that I just loved was not going to come off as I had hoped.

I went into a tailspin.

And then I remembered that there was this women's quartet a few members of which were in my church. I called the one who knew me the most. And I told her the scenario. "Oh, Roger, I want to help. This sounds amazing. The only thing that we could sing, without practice is Sarah McLaughlin's 'The Arms of an Angel'."

I said, I'll get back to you.

I went to see my music director. I told him, "These women can sing 'Arms of An Angel'." He started laughing. He could not stop smiling.

"Roger, let me tell you the story that I'm going to read right before we need a musical piece. Let me tell you the scene that I'll read. It's towards the end of the play and it will be the last part of our service. It is at Matthew's funeral. The Westboro Baptist Church is there, protesting, with hateful signs stating that Matt's in Hell, that kind of thing. And God hates. . . . Just awful signs. Awful protests. And so, knowing this was going to happen, a bunch of Matthew Shepard's friends, wore white robes, and wore huge angel wings to block the family from seeing the protesters. That's the story I'm telling right before they sing, 'In the Arms of An Angel'."

At the service there were tears and tears when that scene was read and those four women closed the service with the perfect song, "Arms of An Angel."

"All will be well," Julian of Norwich wrote. *All manner of things will be well.* I was freaking out thinking that my service was done. It was surely over. I learned the value of asking for help, and trusting the process, and seeking collaboration. It all turned out.

Prayer

May today there be peace within.

May you trust God that you are exactly where you are meant to be.

May you not forget the infinite possibilities that are born of faith.

May you use those gifts that you have received, and pass on the love that has been given to you.

May you be content knowing you are a child of God.

Let this presence settle into your bones, and allow your soul the freedom to sing, dance, praise and love.

It is there for each and every one of us.
Amen.
(Attributed to Teresa of Avila)

Reflection Questions

When have you been in a situation where you thought that you would never survive? A time where you felt like it would not end up even remotely okay, and then you not only survived but found that indeed all was well?

Eschatology is the study of last things. Some people think really complicated things will happen when the world ends. Others just think we die, and there is nothing beyond this one life. What do you think?

What are the infinite possibilities for you that are born of faith?

Kenosis / Solidarity

*Beloved, let us love one another; for love is of God,
and he who loves is born of God and knows God.
He who does not love does not know God; for God is
love." 1 John 4:7–8*

When I first read Bonhoeffer:
There remains an experience
of incomparable value.

We have learned to see
for once
the great events of
world history
from the perspective
from below—

of those who suffer,
the outcast,
the reviled,
the tortured,
the powerless,
the maltreated.

When I first read that
I thought about
those people,
those others,

the ones on the wrong side
of the tracks,

Imprisoned
Enslaved
Forgotten.

Those *other* people, indeed!

Allow me, dear reader,
to show you my superman cape,
my Ubermensch cape!

Roger saves the day!

What I didn't realize,
foolish youth,
Was that I had to identify
And acknowledge
and name
the parts of me that were

Outcast,
Tortured,
Reviled,
Powerless,
Enslaved,
Forgotten.

And only once I grieved

and wailed
And cried out,

why God, why?

Only then could I let go,
engage in the deep action
of kenosis, the very heart
of the Jesus project,

in order that I might be filled
with the humility and self-awareness
Necessary
To be in solidarity,
with even one other person,

whose dignity reflected
the very *alterity* of God.

Prayer

In the moments of our deepest fear,
may we find strength for the journey
and courage.

In the moments of our confusion and uncertainty,
may we find clarity —
clarity of heart, clarity of mind,
clarity of spirit.

In the moments when we don't know which way to go,
may the path be found and the courage to take the first step
and the next.

With God's help and grace.
Amen

Reflection Questions

Kenosis is the idea of letting go, emptying, self-emptying. How do
you try to self-empty?

How are you able to walk into your grief?

When have you known courage? Write about it.

The Messiah Among Us

One thing that I have asked of the Lord, that will I seek after: That I may dwell in the house of the Lord forever. Psalm 27:4

It was 1980. I was 14.

I went to a big church, Baptist, lots and lots of people. Big youth group. Big sanctuary. I played a lot of basketball there in the indoor gym. All in the middle of Illinois.

One Wednesday night I was going from one end of the church to the other.

And as I was passing a particular stairway, I saw this mom and dad and two high school daughters I knew. They were Catholic. They had five children. They started attending our church because our youth group was a lot of fun and had a lot of good kids in it.

They were sitting on the stairs and the mother was crying, the father was trying to comfort her while the two daughters just looked on, incredibly sad. I really loved this family. I was alarmed to see them torn apart and bullied and suffering. It was all jarring.

What was happening? The youth group kids spread the word and soon rumors flew and eventually the truth came out. An old, old man without authority and standing in the church led a Bible Study where he said that the anti-Christ would come out of the Vatican. He said the anti-Christ would be a Pope.

This Catholic couple was among the participants, hearing this nonsense. They were there to give their kids a solid youth group. They were probably trying to find a place where the kids wanted to be that would be safe and where they could flourish.

In retrospect, that church was so confusing for me. Individually, the congregants were generous, funny, loving, kind. But as a whole, the church had this nasty streak, when it came to its core theology. God was going to pick some for salvation, and others were going to get a grindy, nasty hell for all eternity.

Legalism and purity and all of this stuff. God was always watching, ready to get mad, ready to get judgmental. Ready to remind me when I tripped up.

It made it a hard place to build trust, to know who I could trust.

There wasn't a lot of grace and generosity, collectively. Individually, they were generous and lovely. Together, that was another story. I've always looked for stories about generosity and grace with one another.

Here is one I love.

Picture an old beautiful monastery in the middle of a gorgeous deep forest. Off the beaten path. Not so easy to find. But word got out that it was a healing place, a liminal place, a thin place. And folks found their way to it, to restore their spirits, to pray, to be in the sacred silence.

Of late, however, the monks were at each other's throats. Jealousy and pettiness were the order of the day. People could feel it. Something was off.

The Abbot grew distressed, worried for his brothers and worried for the future of the monastery. He remembered his friend, Abraham, a wise old Jewish rabbi who lived close by.

The Abbot told Rabbi Abraham about his worries. Rabbi listened fully and tended to his old friend. Once the Abbot was done, Rabbi gently said, "May I offer a suggestion?"

"Please. Anything," came the response.

Rabbi said, "As you spoke, I received a vision. A crucially important vision. In the vision I saw that one of the monks is in fact the Messiah."

"What?" The Abbot was energized and confused and started to think: *Who could it be?*

He raced back to the monastery after thanking the Rabbi.

When they heard, the monks grew silent and looked upon the face of one another—truly looked.

The mood began to change. These two started talking again, afraid of slighting the Messiah. Another two put aside their bitterness and sought forgiveness. Each began looking for ways to serve the other, to offer presence, compassion, and healing.

Soon word started spreading, again, that the healing spirit, the peaceful spirit of the monastery was back. People found their way back. Looking for rest, contemplation, and renewal of their spirit.

The place grew in spirit, in depth, and in healing. All because the monks knew in an authentic, real way that the Messiah walked among them.

When I think of the beloved community, I think of this wonderful story. We are invited to see each through the eyes of love and to consider the other the Messiah that is to come.

 Prayer

Give us occasion, O Spirit of Life, to remember what it means to be human and what it means to be a part of the great human adventure. To Life!

All those generations that have come before us—they lived here on this earth too. They sought the common good too. They struggled with wrong and right. They sought too after truth. They too fell short, as we certainly do now. But when they triumphed! What strength. What courage. What they did, reminds us that we can do too. Who can climb the hill of the Lord? It is ours to do, while we have breath.

Lead us not into the idea that we can't now do what others have done. Deliver us from our evasions. Deliver us from our fears.

Keep before us our vision and our high resolve! Join us Holy Spirit in the great adventure, until our eyes can see the brotherhood and sisterhood of all, siblings each, and until the joy lives in our hearts! Amen.

How have you begun the work of reconciling the beliefs that you inherited with the beliefs you have grown into?

If you grew up in a faith community, what was your favorite thing about that?

Graph out, if you will, a timeline of your images of God, of your faith development, of what ultimately matters to you and how those things have changed.

The Light that will Guide You

There is faith, there is hope, and there is love. And love endures. 1st Corinthians 13:13

To earn money during seminary, I worked at the University of Maryland Medical System in the center of Baltimore as an on-call chaplain. I worked Tuesday nights and Friday nights on overnight shifts.

And those of us who slept overnight had to sleep on a futon in a small little office at the back of the chapel.

Some nights, I'd get called to the Emergency Room at 2 or 3 in the morning.

From 11 p.m. until 6 a.m., the chapel went dark on an automatic timer. There was no real way to get the chapel lights on at that time.

Sometimes the light in my office in the back of the dark chapel was on. Sometimes it wasn't. Because I was rushing to get out the office door, often I'd forget to turn the light on as I left for those late-night calls.

When I'd return, the chapel was dark, and the little office with the futon was dark too.

I was tired, a little disoriented, and in the dark, after I had concluded my chaplain duties in the Emergency Department.

I'd enter the chapel, slowly making my way towards the place where I would rest. One foot in front of the other, reaching out for a pew for support occasionally. It felt like a long time that I was walking in the dark, not fully knowing where I was going or even if there would be things that would trip me up along the way.

When I finally opened the door in that office with the futon, there was one thing that guided my way, that helped me find my way, even though I was surrounded by the dark, and uncertain, and afraid.

You see, above the futon there was a little shelf, a little headrest. And on that shelf, there was reading material for the chaplains which included a Bible, a novel, and a book of meditations. Next to those books was a little plastic, glow in the dark praying hands, the kind you buy in the dollar store. The praying hands lit up the room, just enough to find the futon.

The light from those praying hands guided me "home," guided me towards rest, towards a couple hours' rest. Those praying hands helped me find comfort, after a long night of toil and strain.

Those praying hands offered the light that guided me on my way.

Maybe you are walking in the dark right now.

Maybe you can't imagine any kind of light.

Sometimes, when I went back to the chapel, the events at the Emergency Room were of such depth and power that I'd just sit in the dark. In an empty pew, all by myself. Maybe the tears would stream down my face. Maybe I'd sit in silent prayer. The dark was where I needed to be in that moment. God had not abandoned me, as I sat in the dark, though I felt very alone. Hope had not abandoned me, though it was often hard to find. I needed the dark in that moment, and I did not need to rush towards the light in my office. The light might be too blinding. It might be too much.

Right now, maybe you are seeing a bit of light, such as the light that came from those plastic, glow-in-the-dark praying hands. Maybe there are glimpses of light for you and you are filled with an emerging sense of hopefulness, even as you know you will never forget your loss.

Maybe the light is growing stronger for you every day.

Every one of us in the midst of such loss moves at her own pace, at his own pace. Be compassionate. Be gentle. With yourselves, first and foremost.

What I know is that you too have a light that will guide you on your way towards peace, comfort, rest, and the promise and hope of a new day. As Paul wrote, three things accompany us: faith, hope, love and the strongest, the most enduring, the most life giving of those is love.

The love that you are, the love at the very heart of your being, is the light that will guide you to rest and comfort and peace. The love that you have will endure and will never go away.

My deepest hope is that you feel the praying hands and the support of those who love you and wish for you the best.

Prayer

O God, we know there is no place we can be that you are not already there.

We pray that those who feel alone might be comforted this day.

That those who are afraid, might feel courage.

That those who are anxious, might find peace.

And may we each find a way to be your healing hands, your smiling face, your embracing hug so that we might all know comfort and courage and peace.
Amen.

Reflection Questions

How have you learned to walk in the dark?

When you were at your lowest, what helped you get through?

What is the light that you possess and share?

What are your own stories of resilience?

What did you learn about yourself in those stories?

Why Not Totally Turn to Fire?

As the appearance of the rainbow in the clouds on a rainy day, so was the appearance of the surrounding radiance. Such was the appearance of the likeness of the glory of the Lord. And when I saw it, I fell on my face and heard a voice speaking. Ezekiel 1:28

Abbot Lot came to Abbot Joseph and said, "Father, to the best of my ability, I keep my little rule, my little fast, my prayer, meditation, and contemplative silence; and to the best of my ability, I work to cleanse my heart of thoughts; what more should I do?"

The elder rose up in reply, and stretched out his hands to heaven, and his fingers became like ten lamps of fire. He said, "Why not be utterly changed into fire?"

Prayer

My prayer is quite simple.
I desire a spirit of
Resilience and Imagination.

Resilience so I might climb
back on that horse
when I fall.

That I might see the options
right in front of me.
And stop, for once,
knocking on the closed door
and see instead the open
field where I might flourish.

Imagination, so that I can see
what there is to see
of this bruised and beautiful world
from some eternal perspective,
casting off my little petty grievances
for a lot of grace
and love
and compassion.

Resilience and Imagination,
it is said,
make up a heart of ministry,
a heart of contemplation.
Ministry and contemplation
make up a life.

The other part of my prayer is simple too.
That you might know what adds up to the heart of your ministry,
whatever it might be, and to know what makes up
the pieces of your life.

Amen.

Reflection Questions

What is the role of imagination in your faith?

Describe a time when you were on fire, deeply passionate, deeply alive?

What is your ministry in the world? What is your contribution?

Thomas Merton's Last Prayer

I am the vine. You are the branches. We abide in one another. We endure. Jesus. The Gospel of John 15:5

I cannot describe the impact Thomas Merton has made on my life. He was a writer and the child of artists. He lived in New York and as a young man converted to Catholicism and in looking for a depth of spirituality, became a monk. He lived in the Abbey of Gethesmani in Kentucky and wrote about silence, politics, peacemaking, non-violence, and the way of Jesus. He deeply appreciated the Buddhist way as well. Without *New Seeds of Contemplation*, I could not be a Christian or a contemplative, no matter how much I come up short in being both! Merton is my constant companion.

In 1968, the Catholic monk and writer, Thomas Merton was given permission to travel to Asia, to both give talks at a few conferences and to experience the vast wisdom of Asian religious traditions. A month before his death in Bangkok, Merton wrote, "I hope I can bring back to my monastery something of the Asian wisdom with which I am fortunate to be in contact."

At some point in his sojourns, he made a pilgrimage to the Buddhist caves of Polonnaruwa. He encountered a series of Buddhas, "barefoot and undisturbed." "Looking at these figures I was suddenly, almost forcibly jerked clean out of the habitual, half-tied vision of things, and an inner clearness, clarity, as if exploding from the rocks themselves, became evident and obvious." (Merton 1975 Revised)

"I know and have seen what I was obscurely looking for. I don't know what else remains but I have now seen and have pierced through the surface and have gone beyond the shadow and the disguise."

His last talk on monasticism and his last prayer are both recorded. His last prayer is an example of the profound power of inter-spiritual and inter-faith relationship. It is easy to find that prayer on the Internet. It begins: O God, we are one with you. I wish everyone in the whole world could read that prayer and absorb it. I encourage you to read it and read it again.

Prayer

In our moments when we feel fragmented,
afraid, shattered, lost,
remind us that we are one.
One with you O mysterious spirit.
One with the great flow of love.
One with each other.
One with the critters and the plants,
the stars and the sea.
None of us is outside the story of love.
None of us is outside grace's embrace.
So strengthen us, bind us together.
Remind us that we come from love,
are made for love, and will undoubtedly,
return to love.
Amen.

Reflection Questions

How have you gone beyond the shadow and the disguise?

What is your habitual, half-tied vision of things? How can you try to
see deeper?

How do we accept one another, wholeheartedly, fully, completely?

What inter-spiritual or interfaith relationships have you cultivated?

Sing, Sing, Sing

Break forth into a shout of joy, you mountains,
O forest, and every tree in it. Isaiah 49:13

I know where you're headed.

I have seen the old lady, sitting next to the bedside, as her husband of many years dies. She is holding his hand. Her head is tucked into his armpit. She knows that smell, his scent, in the way that she knows how to put one foot in front of another. She knows his scent in the way that she knows the English word for tree or moon or sun.

I have seen her cry into his chest, eyes closed. No words left to say. I have seen the nurse gently put a hand on the old lady's shoulder and whisper words of compassion and love, though they have only known one another for a few days or even a few hours.

I have seen the old lady collapse into the arms of her sister when she walks in the room, into the arms of her brother, or her neighbor. A kiss on the forehead and a seat next to hers.

And, then, just like that, in the midst of the tears and the good-byes, I have seen the brother say, "You remember those Friday night card games? How he drank a bit too much and told the same joke week after week? Always lost, but kept the party going."

And she responds, "How many times we listened to Buck Owens and Loretta Lynn. The same albums, over and over. He loved Bakersfield. Home is home. Oh, he'd sing, sing, sing."

And the brother/neighbor/sister recalls something from one of those nights and they howl in laughter.

I know why the humanist exists. I know why the humanist finds so much mystery in this crazy human existence. That we can laugh and cry and remember and make meaning and find hope is enough.

I know why Carl Sandburg, that divine poet, wrote one poem after another as a liturgy, a high prayer, to the beauty of the human spirit, its resilience and power and vulnerability.

And I have walked in on 30 people huddled in a small ICU room singing in Spanish about the suffering heart of Jesus and the crying eyes of Mary and I have felt God there. And I have prayed with a parent and their priest and his seminarian the Lord's Prayer in Lebanese and I have felt the stirrings of a love so profound that it would not possibly let me or anyone else go.

I know why the theist exists, mystery upon mystery, grace upon grace.

One day, you too, will be the old lady, sitting bedside. You too will be the old man.

I know where you're headed.

We are born. We die.

But maybe humanist you are not there yet. Sing your liturgical songs about the mystery at the heart of human life.

Maybe you are not there yet theist. Sing your songs of wonder and awe.

Advent is upon us. And the only adequate response is to sing, sing, sing.

 Prayer

Shine on.
Keep singing.
Keep bearing witness.

Do not grow tired. A great cloud of witnesses cheer you on.
The road can feel long. The way unclear.
The world can seem more bruised and broken
than we might wish it to be. Do not grow weary, especially of doing
good.

As the sacred text says:
So let's not get tired of doing what is good. At just the right time we
will reap a harvest of blessing if we don't give up.

Do not give up. You are on a roll.
You are full of vitality and energy now.

May it be said of you: He spent his life building up a vision of what
he believed in.
She gave her all for the cause of unity and love and grace.
They came to live out loud.

Keep looking for the world's beauty. It is there.

You are keepers of that word of hope. You are bearers, like Mary, of
that good news.
The divine shines through all the time. You are here to help people
figure out where to look, not what to see, but where to look.

That is your good gift.

So Shine on.

Keep singing.

Keep bearing witness.

Amen.

Reflection Questions

What is the soundtrack of your spiritual life?

Make a "mix tape" of your favorite songs that track your spiritual life.

How are you like Mary, the bearer of the good news?

On Staying Sane in a Time of Great Divisiveness

Blessed are the ones who have grown beyond themselves and have seen through their separations.
Psalm 1:1

Sometimes the US seems like it is in the midst of a cold civil war. It is a challenge to stay centered in the midst of so much division and fear. A challenge, yes, but not impossible. I share a few ideas on how to stay grounded and act with integrity, especially for those who are in the midst of the action, regardless of your political persuasions and loyalties.

1. Don't Hunt Every Rabbit

We are hyper-connected with the advent of 24-hour news cycles, social media, and cell phones. This connectedness can be a blessing. Like me, perhaps you've reengaged with long lost friends, not to mention awful/amazing Dad jokes. Nonetheless, there is a downside.

In the weeks leading up to an election day you may get 20 daily appeals to donate to a favorite cause or politician. Politicians will constantly toss up topics and themes to see what lands with key constituents. Pollsters and broadcasters will create an urgent sense of a horse race. Talking heads will clamor for your attention. Your brain will be overwhelmed: *What will it cost me to engage? What will it mean for me to not engage?*

Remember, the hunter who chases two rabbits catches neither one. Figure out a strategy to engage with the news. Don't get caught in the frenzy, on social media, via email, or on television. Strategize to make the most of your time. Take a media Sabbath as you need. You are not here to jump down every rabbit hole.

2. Keep with Your Practices

If you are trying to not hunt down every rabbit, it is important that you keep up your spiritual practices. Walking. Praying. Running. Yoga. Meditation. *Lectio Divina.* It doesn't much matter, just keep it up. Fear is all around us. And on all sides, folks will attempt to exploit your fear.

Regardless which tradition it emerges from, your practice is designed to center love and compassion and downgrade fear. So, keep doing whatever you are doing. And if you want to impact an election, and you find yourself too busy to practice, practice twice as much! In the Christian tradition, St. Paul writes, "For God did not give us a spirit of cowardice, but rather a spirit of power, love and self-discipline." How do we access this spirit of love in the face of enormous uncertainty? Our practices.

3. Know Your Story

You became engaged in political life—as a citizen, a voter, an activist—for some deeply important reason. The more that you know what motivates you to act, the more you will act from an authentic place. The more you know your story and what animates it, the more you'll find compassion-satisfaction and life-giving activity. Have you been to a church soup kitchen and the volunteer dishing soup is curmudgeonly with their neighbors in need? They've forgotten why they are doing what they are doing. Your genesis story is the oxygen that the blood needs to give life, politically and socially. Your genesis story on why you've become engaged in politics is your beating heart. Know your story. Know its lessons. And keep it in the front of your mind. Let that story of pain, resilience, triumph, and solidarity drive your engagement.

4. Keep Your Eye on the Vision

Build a vision/icon board, with your "cloud of witnesses" in order to stay focused on what matters to you. The icons will call forth your deepest aspirations and values. They will focus your attention. It isn't that these icons were perfect. They memorably responded to their times with creativity, imagination, and passion. That is what you are called to do as well. My vision board includes Oscar Romero, Dorothy Day, Bonhoeffer, Howard Thurman, Carl Sandburg, MLK. Who is on yours? Build it!

5. Stay Connected to the "Other"

"In a democracy, there are no enemies."
In a divisive season, you may be tempted to use language that dehumanizes those with whom you have significant disagreement. This is a trap. Resist the easy temptation. Instead, stay close to at least one person with differing opinions. Proximity will enable you to see the humanity of those with whom you disagree, understand their fears, and hear their concerns. And in the process, you may find some common ground. This will help you to stay compassionate. You can retain your strong sense of right and wrong and simultaneously come to appreciate their worldview more.

Look, I am a hospital chaplain. When I knock on the door of a patient room, I have no idea what I might find. Fear, anger, fatigue, regret, an amazing love story. How do I step into that room? I stay humble, curious, and courageous. I bring to mind times when I have been nauseous and frightened, to realize again that we are each a fallible, decaying, beautiful human. I know I will look like that one day. So, I get as close as I reasonably can. I keep my heart open, my mouth shut, and my ears attentive. *What do you want me to learn about you today? What do you want me to see?* Humanizing the "other" takes humility, curiosity, and plenty of courage.

Protect your heart. In this season and always. Stay connected to your best self, your sacred source, and to all humanity.

Thomas Merton told us, once and for all,

"Life is this simple: we are living in a world that is absolutely transparent and the divine is shining through it all the time. This is not just a nice story or a fable, it is true" (Merton 1965).

God bless you, one and all.

I am the open road.
I am the wind and the tree.
The leaves, the branches,
the fruit.
I am the new born baby,
crying its first breath.
I am possibility.
I am the trunk and the roots.
I am the old woman,
struggling to get out of her chair,
cane in hand. One more walk.
I am the old man,
lying in bed,
who smiles when his dog comes in the room.
I am the leaf that falls
in September,
the snowflake in December.
I am new life,

the second chance,
the third chance.
I am the house in the open prairie
and the kids playing in the yard.

Roger Butts

For Further Reading

This book highlights a number of individuals who sought to deepen our sense of a life lived fully in the spirit.

To learn more:

James Baldwin
The Fire Next Time
The Devil Finds Work

Dietrich Bonhoeffer
Letters and Papers from Prison
The Cost of Discipleship

Dorothy Day
The Long Loneliness

James Finley
Merton's Palace of Nowhere

Vincent Harding
Martin Luther King: The Inconvenient Hero

Martin Luther King, Jr.
Stride Toward Freedom: The Montgomery Story,

A Knock At Midnight: Inspiration from the Great Sermons of Reverend Martin Luther King, Jr.

Thomas Merton
Conjectures of a Guilty Bystander
New Seeds of Contemplation
Seven Storey Mountain

Toni Morrison
Playing in the Dark
Beloved

Henri Nouwen
Return of the Prodigal Son
The Wounded Healer
The Road to Peace (edited by John Dear)

Parker Palmer
A Hidden Wholeness: The Journey Toward an Undivided Life

Rachel Naomi Remen
My Grandfather's Blessings: Stories of Strength, Refuge and Belonging

Rumi
The Soul of Rumi: A New Collection of Ecstatic Poems. Coleman Barks

Saint Teresa of Avila
The Interior Castle. New translation and introduction by Mirabai Starr

Carl Sandburg
The Complete Poems of Carl Sandburg.

Howard Thurman
The Growing Edge
Meditations of the Heart

Josiah Ulysses Young III
No Difference in the Fare

Others that point the way:

Cynthia Bourgeault
The Heart of Centering Prayer
The Wisdom Jesus

Walter Brueggemann
The Prophetic Imagination

James Cone
A Black Theology of Liberation
The Cross and the Lynching Tree

Gustavez Guitterez
A Theology of Liberation
On Job

Abraham Joshua Heschel
The Sabbath

Richard Hooper
The Essential Mystics, Poets, Saints and Sages

Tarif Khalidi (ed.)
The Muslim Jesus: Sayings and Stories in Islamic Literature

Carl McColman
The Big Book of Christian Mysticism: The Essential Guide to Contemplative Spirituality

Mary Oliver
New and Selected Poems, Volume 1

Walter Rauschenbush
A Theology for the Social Gospel

Films/Movies

Backs Against the Wall: The Howard Thurman Story

BONHOEFFER: Pastor, Nazi Resister, Martyr. Journey Films

I am Not Your Negro

Revolution of the Heart, Journey Films

Soul Searching, Morgan Atkinson

About the Author

Roger Butts is a Staff Chaplain at a hospital system in Colorado Springs. A graduate of Wesley Theological Seminary in D.C., he is ordained in the Unitarian Universalist tradition. He is a long-time member of the Unitarian Universalist Christian Fellowship and the International Thomas Merton Society. After serving two UU congregations as senior minister, he traveled for a year organizing against the death penalty throughout Colorado. When he can, he sits with the Springs Mountain Sangha (Buddhist) at Colorado College. His prayers and an essay have been published in a number of anthologies from Skinner House Books. He is also a contributing writer for Contemplative Light. His writings have been published in the Boulder Daily Camera, the CS Gazette, and the Quad City Times. For many years he was a board member of the local branch of the NAACP and the Greenberg Center for Learning and Tolerance in Colorado Springs. He is married to Marta Fioriti, a minister in the Black Forest of Colorado Springs. They have three teenagers and a black lab.

He believes humor and grace will save us all.

Find out more at GracePointPublishing.com/roger-butts

Visit GraceLight Press online at GraceLightPress.com

Printed in Great Britain
by Amazon

82885713R00150